T

The Isı

How the U.S., China, and Japan
Influenced the Forming of a New Nation

Pacific Atrocities Education

TAIWAN

The Israel of the East

How the U.S., China, and Japan Influenced the Forming of a New Nation

LUKE DIEP-NGUYEN

TAIWAN

The Israel of the East

How the U.S., China, and Japan
Influenced the Forming of a New Nation

Copyright © 2020 by Luke Diep-Nguyen

Editor:
David Trout

All rights reserved. Printed in the United States of America. No part of this book may be reproduced in any manner whatsoever without written permission except in the case of brief quotations embodied in critical articles and reviews. For information, address Pacific Atrocities Education, 730 Commercial Street, San Francisco, CA 94108.

Paperback ISBN: 978-1-947766-26-6

E-book ISBN: 978-1-947766-13-6

Table of Contents

Acknowledgement

This book would not have been completed or granted the large volume of information without the help of a few individuals. First, I would like to thank Ellen Hickman, granddaughter of Kay Hickman, an individual discussed in my book, who provided a transcript and audio recording of a conversation with her grandmother which provided a fascinating and insightful look into Taiwanese life under Japanese occupation. I would also like to acknowledge my supervisor at Pacific Atrocities Education, Jenny Chan, who recognized my capabilities to tell a story of this magnitude and helped me connect with interesting sources such as Ms. Hickman and other sources on Taiwan. Next, I would like to thank my mentor, Augusta Weaver, for helping grow my writing techniques and providing constant support. Finally, I would like to thank my parents, Tin Hoang Nguyen and Cynthia Diep, and my brother, Arthur Diep-Nguyen, who supported me through this process. There are many friends and family who also supported and motivated me to finish this sometimes exhausting process. To all of them, I express my deepest thanks and gratitude.

Introduction

Following World War II, the United States became a major political and military superpower. The U.S. used profits from wartime production to allow it to economically and militarily assist democratic European and Asian countries to combat the rise of communism. The United States emerged as a world peacekeeper, becoming a founding member of the United Nations, an organization created to promote international peace and security while preventing other countries from becoming global threats or committing international crimes. The U.S. also participated in creating a Western Alliance to provide political, economic, and military support to combat the spread of communism and prevent Western European countries from being taken over by communism.

President Harry Truman, at the onset of the Cold War, established the Truman Doctrine, a foreign policy program designed to defend all democratic nations from the perceived threat of communism. It also backed U.S. involvement in international affairs and conflicts. The Truman Doctrine's primary cause was the British Government refusing to support the Greek Government against the Greek Communist Party, spurring Truman to request permission to aid Greece and Turkey against communism. Truman believed that the Soviet Union and Greek Communist Party would influence and control Greek policies that would affect their relations with the United States. President Truman provided more than $341 million in aid to Greece and Turkey and dispatched U.S. personnel to provide military and political assistance to these countries. The Truman Doctrine argued for a more proactive role in the struggle against communism and international affairs in general.[1]

While Truman attempted to focus on controlling communism in Europe with containment and Marshall Plan policies, the Central Intelligence Agency had been analyzing and reporting on the situation in Asia, particularly China, to look into possible threats such as the rise of communism in Pacific Asian countries.[2] In China, Mao Zedong founded the Communist Party in 1927 in Shanghai. The Communist Party initially worked with the Nationalist Party as a part of the Northern Expedition of 1926-1927 to oppose the warlords of China. The Nationalist Party betrayed the Communists during the White Terror in 1927, also known as the Shanghai Massacre, which killed and expelled thousands of Communist Chinese. This incident led to the start of the civil war between the Nationalist Party, or Kuomintang, under Chiang Kai-shek, and Mao's Communist Party. When the

---

[1] President Truman's Message to Congress; March 12, 1947; Document 171; 80th Congress, 1st Session; Records of the United States House of Representatives; Record Group 233; National Archives.

[2] "Kennan and Containment, 1947—Office of the Historian." https://history.state.gov/milestones/1945-1952/kennan. Accessed October 16, 2019.

Japanese invaded Manchuria in 1931 and threatened China with invasion, Chiang was forced to cooperate with the Chinese Communists to unite against the Japanese. While the Nationalist Army exhausted its forces and resources while defending many of their cities against a superior Japanese military, the communists retreated into the mountains and focused on influencing highland and rural citizens, and building their resources. The war allowed Mao to gain support through positive influence and opposing the dictatorial manner of Chiang and his Nationalist government.

The end of the war allowed the Nationalist Party, with assistance from the U.S., to retake previously Japanese-occupied regions. After the Japanese surrendered, Chiang and Mao had multiple meetings to discuss post-war China and its governments. While the parties acknowledged an emphasis on a singular military force and fair treatment of all political parties, the tension of hatred and mistrust of their respective adversaries led to the outbreak of the civil war between the Communists and Nationalists.[3]

By 1948, the CIA had provided multiple detailed reports analyzing China and the dire consequences of a communist takeover of China's government. The CIA viewed the Nationalist government in China as necessary because of its role as the stabilizer of political influence in the Far East, essentially responsible for maintain-

---

[3] "The Chinese Revolution of 1949—Office of the Historian." https://history.state.gov/milestones/1945-1952/chinese-rev. Accessed October 20, 2019.

ing democracy in the Pacific Asia region. The U.S. feared that if China fell to communism, it could spread across Asia. Unfortunately, the Nationalist government had been unstable, benefitting the influence of communism in China. It was made clear, according to the CIA report, that, by 1948, Nationalist China had gradually become more vulnerable and weakening militarily, politically, and economically.

In the meantime, the communist military had steadily secured itself, politically and militarily, with support from the Soviet Union. The Nationalist government made Chiang Kai-shek their president due to his victory against the Japanese and substantial anti-communist views. The U.S. provided President Chiang advice on reforming his government to solve China's dissolving economic, political, and military situations. President Chiang did not consider these suggestions because he felt that the public would not support these reforms.[4]

The CIA also used another analytical report on the ongoing Chinese Civil War to understand possibilities and hypotheses on the current situation in China, war outcomes, and the impact on China's future. Due to its political and military disadvantages, it was clear that the Nationalist Party had a high chance of losing the war. Although numerically superior to the Communist military, the Nationalist army consistently lost against the Communist Party, militarily and politically.

---

[4] Central Intelligence Agency to Department of State, Report, July 22, 1948, CIA-RDP78-01617A003200210001-2, CREST System, General CIA Records.

Many Nationalist troops defected due to the loss of respect and trust in Chiang and the Nationalist Government. President Chiang and the Nationalist government, as understood through the CIA reports, were also seen as incompetent and corrupt, leading to substantial social and political issues that were handled poorly. To the CIA, significant evidence existed that Chiang would be displaced and that the Nationalist government would be eliminated. Although this also supported a strong belief in a communist control of China, there was an understanding that, although anti-imperialists, the Communists would have economic issues if they did not cooperate or interact with western powers.

Since 1947, the CIA and the Chiang's Nationalist Government watched developments in Manchuria and Taiwan as possible settling positions for Chiang and his supporters should they lose to the Communists who, by this time, were very likely to win. Chiang heavily opposed communism and therefore supported that the idea that, if he lost, his supporters and anti-communists would leave China to build a new government that would continue to oppose Mao and his Communist Party.[5] In October 1949, Mao took over Beijing, the capital of China, and established the People's Republic of China government. By the end of 1949, Chiang, his supporters, and nearly 2 million Chinese under the Nationalist government or anti-communists would evacuate to Taiwan.

[5] Central Intelligence Agency to Department of State, Report, November 19, 1948, CIA-RDP78-01617A003200040001-1, CREST System, General CIA Records.

Taiwan's development as a state under the Nationalist government draws close similarities to the creation and establishment of Israel in 1948. It is essential to look at the establishment and early developments of Israel to understand the close comparisons between these two nations.

In 1917, during the First World War, the British Government presented a public statement written by Foreign Secretary Arthur Balfor, known as the Balfour Declaration, which declared that the British "favour the establishment in Palestine of a national home for the Jewish people."[6] The end of World War II led to millions of displaced Jewish people from thousands of European concentration camps and other discriminated groups who were taken from their homes, most of which were either destroyed or re-possessed during the war.. Without homes for many Holocaust survivors, it was decided by Jewish leaders in Europe that the Jewish refugees could relocate to Palestine, where an already minority Jewish community was established following the Balfour Declaration.

While the U.S. supported this claim, in 1945 President Franklin D. Roosevelt favored negotiating with both the Jewish and Arabs in Israel before intervening. The British, on the other hand, opposed a two-state system where Palestine would split into a state for the Jewish refugees and displaced people, and another for Arabs. They also opposed the unlimited immigration of Jewish refugees, while supporting the issues to maintain

---

[6] Arthur Balfor. Balfour Declaration of 1917, 1917.
Retrieved from https://avalon.law.yale.edu/20th_century/balfour.asp.

a positive relationship with the Arabs to promote political and economic benefits.

Following the Second World War, newly appointed President Truman arranged meetings with foreign affairs experts to further analyze and understand the Palestine situation. In 1946, Truman formed a cabinet committee with Assistant Secretary of State, Dr. Henry Grady, to discuss the future of Palestine with Britain's cabinet committee. In May, Truman publicly proclaimed favoring relocating displaced Jewish people to Palestine. He also approved of the establishment of a separate Jewish state in the region. The transfer would begin with the movement of 100,000 Jewish refugees to Palestine.[7]

During the next year, the United Nations Special Commission on Palestine studied the partition of Palestine into two states. On November 29, 1947, the U.N. formed Resolution 181, or the United Nations Partition Plan for Palestine, which outlined the separation of Palestine into the Jewish State of Israel and the Arab States of Palestine. The resolution instructed the rights of each state and how each state would act and cooperate with other nations.[8] On May 14, 1948, David Ben-Gurion, head of the Jewish Agency, announced the creation of

[7] "Creation of Israel, 1948—Office of the Historian—United States..." https://history.state.gov/milestones/1945-1952/creation-israel. Accessed October 17, 2019.

[8] U.N. General Assembly, *Future Government of Palestine*, November 29, 1947, A/RES/181, available at: https://www.refworld.org/docid/3b00f1950.html [accessed October 18, 2019]

the State of Israel. President Truman announced his recognition of the new state that same day.

Dr. Benjamin Shwardan, a Middle Eastern Studies professor, wrote about the re-emergence of the Jewish State of Israel in the Journal of Educational Sociology. The Jewish people, as Dr. Shwardan explained, wanted to reclaim their original land after years of oppression. Dr. Shwardan believed that the inclination to retrieve their property was "nationalistic revivals and the emergence of new states in Europe; the general deterioration in the Jewish economic position and the intensification of anti-Semitism... and the spread of secularism."[9]

Even before Resolution 181 and World War I, the Jewish people were still driven to Palestine, which they believed to be given to them by God. Dr. Shwardan discussed the unification and promotion of Modern Zionism and the establishment of an independent Jewish state. He believes that this idea originated in 1897 with the creation of the Zionist Organization, which promoted the idea of a new independent Jewish state. Its founder, Dr. Theodor Herzl, also helped the rise of the World Zionist Council. After approval of the Balfour Declaration, the Jewish people began their movement into, and instituted their Jewish community in, Palestine. Starting small with a population of only 50,000, before the end of World War II there were 700,000 more Jewish immigrants. The Jewish Palestine community not only grew

[9] Shwadran, Benjamin. "The Emergence of the State of Israel." The Journal of Educational Sociology 22, no. 3 (1948): 163-70. doi:10.2307/2263514, p. 163-164.

in size, it also developed a Jewish agricultural, commercial, educational, cultural, and social evolution.[10]

It is essential to understand the developments of Israel to follow the progress of Taiwan. In China, President Chiang and his Nationalist supporters were defeated by the Communist Army, while many Jewish people in Europe were forced to seek refuge in Palestine to avoid oppression.

This book chronicles the developments and growth of Taiwan before the arrival of the Nationalist and into its changes following the establishment of the Chinese Nationalist government. Formosa not only changed culturally and industrially, its natives had been persecuted and abused by many colonizers, from Japan during the early 20th century to the new Chinese settlers. In the present day, the Palestinian struggle to adapt to sharing their state with the massive influx of Jewish refugees is well known, yet the public has forgotten the Formosan plight following the arrival of Chinese Nationalists.

The date of Taiwan's establishment has been widely debated. While many believe that Taiwan officially formed after the establishment of the Taiwan National Government, others believe that establishment corresponded with the formation of the Republic of China in 1912. This argument is still debated today.

---

[10] Ibid., p. 165.

Chapter 1:

Background of Formosa

Geography

It is crucial to analyze Formosa's geography and natives to understand the importance of Formosa and its native population under foreign influences.

Formosa is an island of approximately 15,000 sq. miles, with forested mountain ranges, lowlands, plateaus, and ravines, surrounded by coral reefs. Formosa is connected with the Fujian province at roughly 2000 meters underwater. Volcanoes and igneous rocks rose 1500 feet above sea level, and corals were found on mountain peaks 2000 feet above sea level. Many Formosan months and seasons have extreme weather, particularly in the summer months. June, July, and August often become extremely hot, with droughts and temperatures as high as a hundred degrees. Torrential typhoons and tropical storms are very frequent in August and September. During the winter months of December, January, and February, rain lasts for days or weeks. Mild, tropical weather usually occurs during spring months, as well as in October and November.

The seasonal climates are critical to understanding the rise in frequency of trading and expeditions during certain times of the year.[11] Formosa attracted many merchants after a series of expeditions, due to their interest in attaining natural resources and food supplies. Formosa's natural resources included coal, natural gas, petroleum, salt, sulfur, iron, and gold. It thrived from a wide variety of vegetation and fruits that became essential sources of tradable products. Formosa attracted many explorers with its lush trees and flowers that produced essential foods such as rice, sweet potatoes, yams, plums, bananas, and oranges. The island nation also produced tobacco and tea, among the most influential trade goods at the time.[12]

All of these items were extremely important for redistribution within the nation in or for trade with other merchants who used Formosa as their trading center. The increased demand for these products transformed Formosa into a crucial trading center among Pacific Asian countries, attracting many future European expeditions. Trade traffic with foreign merchants and communities became profitable to those using Formosa as a trading center, but also had a significant effect on the natives.

---

[11] Presbyterian missionary George Mackay lived and traveled to Formosa from 1871 until his death in 1901. He would research Formosa on its people and its geography during his time in Formosa. The understanding of the profits of Chinese supplies in Formosa and religious expansion was taken from his studies in the 19th century. Mackay, G. L., & MacDonald, J. A. *From far Formosa: The island, its people and missions*. New York: F. H. Revell Co., 1896, p. 42.

[12] Mackay, G. L., & MacDonald, J. A. *From far Formosa,* p. 66-71.

Formosan natives were divided into two categories: lowland autochthon and mountainous autochthon. Both native categories could be divided into smaller tribal groups, depending on their descriptive anthropological traits and geographical positioning. Lowland aboriginals comprised of fourteen different tribes, and the mountainous natives, nine.[13]

Taiwanese natives[14]

[13] Wang, I-Shou. "Cultural Contact and the Migration of Taiwan's Aborigines: A Historical Perspective." In China's Island Frontier: Studies in the Historical Geography of Taiwan, edited by Knapp Ronald G., 29-51. Honolulu: University of Hawai'i Press, 1980. doi: 10.2307/j.ctv9zckx5.7, p. 30.

[14] Taiwanese aborigines, from Olfert Dapper (1670): *Gedenkwaerdig bedryf, Olfert Dapper—University Library Nijmegen,* https://it.wikipedia.org/wiki/File:Dapper_-_1670_-_Gedenkwaerdig_bedryf_-_UB_Radboud_Uni_Nijmegen_-_180148540_038_%28cropped%29.jpg

Similar to the treatment of other native groups under colonial rule, the Chinese treated Formosan natives harshly. During their settlement, the Chinese bartered with the natives, yet forced natives off their own lands into areas inhabited by other tribes.[15] While exploring the island and building trade centers, the Chinese wanted to provide for their community in Formosa. This community would be built on towns and villages, which tended to be safer and more pleasant to the Chinese than the countryside. These towns also created an expanded work environment for Chinese workers such as blacksmiths, silversmiths, jewelers, weavers, and tailors.

In Formosa, farmers became the most important and esteemed workers due to their importance in the Chinese-Formosan economy. They produced goods essential to all domestic and foreign consumers and traders. The most cultivated resource in Formosa was rice, followed by tea, which became the most profitable products. Tea, particularly, became in high demand due to European and American influence and its spread among Pacific Asian nations. Other products cultivated in farms included sugar cane, sweet potatoes, onions, and other consumable vegetation.

Along with workers, traders, and merchants, Presbyterian missionary George Mackay recorded that at least 3 million Chinese settled in Formosa by the end of the 19th century. They not only built towns, they worked on farms and spread their religion to convert the native population.[16]

---

[15] Mackay, G. L., & MacDonald, J. A. *From far Formosa*, p. 103

[16] Ibid., p. 113-116.

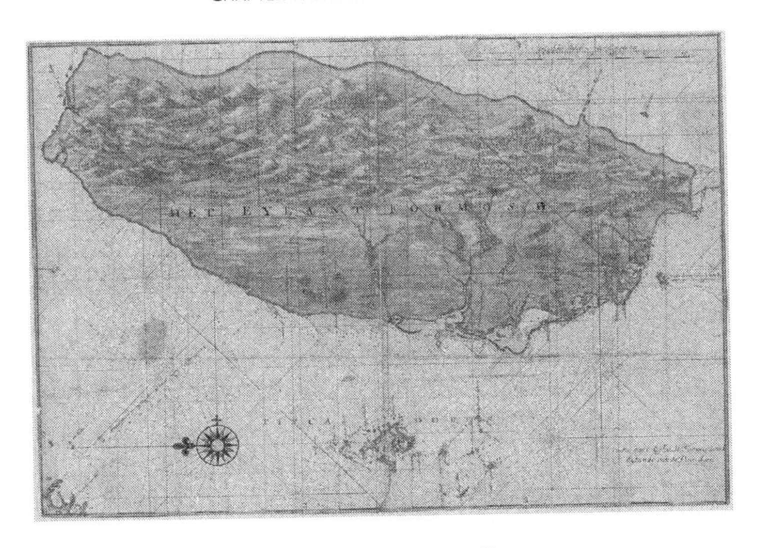

Dutch Map of Taiwan 1640[17]

History

The first accounts of Formosa were delineated by an early 6th century Chinese expedition. Chinese scholars believed that the natives were part of the Loochoo people from the Loochoo Islands, now known as the Ryukyu Islands. As a result, the aboriginals were known by Chinese historians as Lonkius. During a second Chinese expedition, it was discovered that Malayan natives also traveled and arrived in Formosa between the two teams. Little documentation followed the second expedition

[17] 1640 Map of Formosa, Johannes Vingboons—Nationaal Archief, Den Haag source. Copied from Chinese Wikipedia. Original source: npm.gov.tw https://commons.wikimedia.org/wiki/File:1640_Map_of_Formosa-Taiwan_by_Dutch_%E8%8D%B7%E8%98%AD%E4%BA%BA%E6%89%80%E7%B9%AA%E7%A6%8F%E7%88%BE%E6%91%A9%E6%B2%99-%E8%87%BA%E7%81%A3.jpg

until the beginning of the Ming Dynasty. The Ming Dynasty reported their historical discoveries in a series of annals known as the Ming Shilu, which became the most significant historical record of the Ming Dynasty. During the rise of the Ming Dynasty, the Chinese launched a series of expeditions under Admiral Yang-Tsing to study Formosa and the Loochoo people. These expeditions discovered that Formosan natives were distinct from the Loochoo and seen as foreigners by the Loochoo people. As such, more teams were sent to Formosa to examine further and understand them, but it would not be known as Formosa until the 16th century.

In 1430, a eunuch officer of the Ming Court, Wan-so-ho, landed on Formosa while avoiding a harsh storm. Unaware of the island nation at the time, he discovered that the natives tended to him and regarded him favorably. When Wan-so-ho reported his findings to the emperor, he brought back a multitude of herbs discovered to be very important medicinal supplements. Following further expeditions, Formosans had many encounters with pirates and traders off the coast, notably Chinese and Japanese, because of the importance and value of the island chain. Japanese pirates began raiding Chinese coastal towns and villages primarily along the Fujian coast. Pirates dealt so much damage to the coastal communities that the Ming emperor was forced to limit trading and connections with neighboring island ports.

During the late 16th century, after numerous expeditions and findings from traders and explorers, China and Japan began to view the commercial and political importance of Formosa. While the two countries relationship had grown tense due to the raids, Formosa became a neutral ground with ports that allowed all nations to trade and distribute goods, mediated without distributions or imposition of taxes. Formosa also started attracting merchants to engage with the movement of the rising profits from its trading ports. While most merchants conducted business only with traders of their own countries, Japan granted specific clearances for merchants from certain Japanese towns such as Nagasaki, Kyoto, and Sakai to trade with other countries. Traders eventually made Tainan, the Formosan capital, the trading center and primary port for Japan, China, Luzon, and Siam.[18]

The importance of Formosa slowly grew because of its geographical location in the Pacific. Formosa is located off the coast of China's Fujian province, which provided a major central trading point for both China and Japan, two major economic Asian countries. While it started as an exploration center for finding natural resources, Formosa became a trading center for China and Japan to do business, which attracted traders and merchants from other countries, which in turn transformed Formosa into a profitable commercial center.

The first Europeans to arrive on Formosa were the Portuguese. They discovered Formosa during an expedition to China in 1514. In the early 1500s, many Portuguese that arrived and explored Formosa were mer-

---

[18] It is important to note that this is research done by James Wheeler Davidson when he visited Formosa in the 19th century. Davidson, J. W. *The island of Formosa, past and present*, p. 1-7.

chants, explorers, and ambassadors on their way to China and were allowed to organize their centers on Formosa to facilitate trade with China. In 1590, it was recorded that the Portuguese formed their settlement in Keelung, where they named the island, Formosa. Other Portuguese settlers also created names such as "Ilha Formosa," which translates to "beautiful isle." While Portuguese settlers informally named it "Formosa," the Dutch *officially* mapped and named the island Formosa.

The Dutch launched their first Pacific expedition in 1595, which arrived in Java with the goal of establishing a Pacific trading business. Starting with their first expedition to Macao and the Penghu Islands, the Dutch and Dutch East India Company led a series of voyages in an attempt to open trade in the East Asian and Southeast Asian regions.

Feeling threatened, the Chinese and Portuguese sent several Chinese junks to engage with the Dutch fleet. Until 1607, the Dutch continued efforts to establish themselves in Pacific islands off the coast of China to capitalize on the high commercial traffic. After failing to reach Penghu islands, Formosa, or Macao due to pressure from Portuguese and Chinese soldiers and junks, the Dutch halted all expeditionary attempts and focused on exploiting the natural minerals in the Dutch East Indies.[19]

In 1622, the Dutch sent Captain Reyerson to attempt to engage in negotiating trade with the Chinese. Although failing to reach Macau or China, Captain Reyerson came upon the southern end of Formosa and was able to organ-

[19] Davidson, J. W. *The island of Formosa*, p. 9-11.

ize business with the nearby Chinese inhabitants. While Reyerson built a trading center in Formosa, Dutch fleets settled on the Pescadores Islands, now known as the Penghu islands, to assist in supplying the Dutch establishment in Formosa and expand trade in the area. The Dutch used yachts to support their shipping and trading business. In the latter half of 1622 and beginning of 1623, Dutch ships frequently engaged with Chinese junks attempting to enter Chinese ports and coastline to open up trade with the Chinese, but frequently lost due to Chinese numerical and military superiority.

In October 1623, Commander Reyerson changed the failing forced trade tactics to a more passive strategy. Through examining past failures, Reyerson decided that the Dutch should seek a more natural trading approach and advance peaceful negotiation. Reyerson sent a letter offering friendship to the Chinchew region merchants to avoid any possible threat of hostilities. At the end of October, they sailed under escort to the Chinchew River in the Fukien province and offered a friendly trade agreement. On November 1, merchants from Hokchiu, now Fuzhou, the capital of Fujian (Fukien) province, met with the Dutch on their yachts to discuss the trade agreement. The merchant petitioned their leaders to allow trade with the Dutch.[20]

---

[20] Reverend William Campbell was Scottish Presbyterian missionary who arrived on Formosa in 1871 and wrote extensively on the Dutch history of Formosa using Dutch historical records. Campbell, W. *Formosa Under the Dutch, Described from Contemporary Records.* London. Kegan Paul, Trench, Trubner & Co., Ltd., 1903, p. 27-34.

In 1624, 25,000 Chinese, several Japanese merchants, and Spanish and Portuguese commerce inhabited Formosa. The Chinese and Japanese, holding most claim over the island, gave it to the Dutch in exchange for peaceful commerce since many of the regional islands, such as Macao and the Ryukyus, encountered more hostilities between European and Asian merchants and traders.

Upon creating their government on Formosa, the Dutch immediately increased defenses surrounding the port cities of Tainan and Provintia. Two major defensive strongholds were built on hills overlooking the ports and area surrounding the ports. The defensive fortresses, Fort Zeelandia and Fort Provintia, established an observational and defensive position for the Dutch.[21]

After establishing political control over the island, the Dutch decided to limit the trading permission between China and Japan. Instead, they wanted to trade with China and Japan independently, as their trade. Interests with each nation dictated a change of course. The Dutch exported cargoes of silk, rice, sugar, deerskin, deer horns, and drugs to China, while the Dutch also sent raw silk and sugar to Japan. Dutch Formosa also traded with the Dutch East Indies, present-day Indonesia, specifically their capital of Batavia, present-day Jakarta. Formosa gained a total of $600,000 US gold via these trading partners.

The Dutch, in 1626, began to allow the Spaniards to settle in Northern Formosa.[22] For more than a decade, the Dutch and Spanish harmoniously coexisted and

---

[21] Davidson, J. W. *The island of Formosa*. p. 13.

[22] Ibid., p. 15.

traded with each other. In 1641, however, the Spanish cut off connections with the Portuguese, which the Dutch saw as a potential means to betray the Dutch and attempt to claim their territory in Formosa. As a result of this perceived threat, the Dutch sent a series of military expeditions over the next few months to reclaim the Spanish territory of Formosa.

While the first few attempts failed due to strong Spanish defenses, the Dutch successfully established a foothold on Spanish territory and ultimately prevented supplies and reinforcements, from Manila in the Spanish Philippines, from assisting the Spanish region on Formosa. By 1642, the Spanish were forced off Formosa, virtually cutting off all Spanish trade and commerce with Dutch Formosa.

Dutch Formosa reached the height of prosperity in 1650 by having jurisdiction over almost 300 villages across Taiwan. The Dutch controlled more than 45 native tribes, splitting them into seven districts. Under the Dutch during the 17th century, it was mostly the southwestern Formosan tribes who engaged and were influenced.[23] The Dutch wanted to express a more positive and benevolent relationship with native tribes than the Chinese, with the vital goal of making it easier to extend their jurisdiction, cooperation, and policies on the native population, particularly the Sakkan tribe inhabiting the region surrounding Dutch port cities stationed on Formosa.[24]

---

[23] Wang, I-Shou. "Cultural Contact and the Migration of Taiwan's Aborigines", p. 32.

[24] Davidson, J. W. *The island of Formosa, past, and present: History, people, resources, and commercial prospects*, 1903. p. 13.

Aside from establishing policies and taxes on Formosan tribes, the Dutch also changed the way the tribes cultivated their lands. The Dutch accomplished this by promoting and incentivizing in-migration of Chinese laborers to assist in supplying the nation with animals, tools, seeds, and cash, and participating in cultivating the land they bought to establish settlements. While the Chinese focused on excluding the natives and forming their independent community, the Dutch focused on converting and incorporating the natives into their lifestyle. Through their policies, the Dutch made the natives reliant on imposed taxes, trade, and their culture and institutional system. During Dutch occupation, missionaries settled in Formosa to encourage the native population to convert to Christianity. The Dutch constructed schools, missions, and other institutions that introduced and implemented Western and Christian cultures. For the Dutch, religion, particularly Christianity, was an essential factor in assimilating Formosans into their culture. While the Dutch Formosan government left natives to their own devices with respect to liberty and original customs, they still expected them to pay taxes and follow Dutch policies. Dutch schools and missions, most of which were Christian, helped convert and teach natives Christianity, basing the education of native children on Dutch culture and customs. As the Dutch further expanded across Taiwan, schools and Christian missions also spread, facilitating conversion, and providing government aid to the native population.

While the Dutch expanded control and influence across Formosa, China had entered a stage of political turmoil. The Manchus from the north invaded the Ming Dynasty, forcing 12 Chinese provinces into capitulation and situating their new empire under the Shunzhi emperor. The newly established Qing Dynasty seized control over the capital and crushed all native rebellions. In the wake of the usurpation, a Fujian native, whose father was a wealthy trade merchant who fought against the Manchus, was forced to flee with his mother to Japan. The Fujian, eventually known as Koxinga, became vengeful of the Manchus and, alongside other Chinese refugees, sought to build a military to seek revenge.

Koxinga, despite having a large naval force, failed to overthrow the Qing Dynasty due to heavy defenses around the capital. After failing to retake any part of China, Koxinga and his remaining forces found interest in Formosa as a potential base to rebuild their rebellion.

In 1661, Koxinga successfully forced the Dutch out of Formosa. Over the course of Formosa's Koxinga dynasty, both the Qing Dynasty and Dutch tried to reclaim the island, but failed. In 1683, the Qing Dynasty succeeded in turning over the Koxinga family, eventually claiming the island as Chinese territory.

In 1684, the Qing Dynasty seized control of Formosa. Under the Qing Dynasty, Formosa would be renamed Taiwan and considered a prefecture. Unlike earlier colonizers who tended to remain along the coasts, ideal for building and maintaining trading ports, and lowlands, which provided fertile farming grounds, the Qing government decided to extend their territory into the mountainous regions. The mountain tribes, fiercer than their lowland counterparts, attacked and instigated numerous uprisings and riots against the Chinese. After sustaining heavy losses and casualties without gaining much, the Qing Dynasty finally backed off and restricted any Chinese from advancing into the mountains. They also blocked immigration to Taiwan from China.

During the late 18th and early 19th century, the Chinese population in Taiwan increased, and they began to overtake and occupy more lowland territories and deltas. When the Qing initially conquered Taiwan in 1684, there were approximately 100,000 Chinese settlements there; within two centuries, the population expanded to over 3 million. Natives who refused to or couldn't migrate into the mountains were integrated and assimilated into Chinese communities and culture. The Chinese also changed the plains for agricultural use during this time period.[25]

Starting in the mid-19th century, more than a half century after the Qing Dynasty occupation, the Chinese began foreign trade by opening ports to British and Spanish merchants. The Chinese primarily exported tea from Formosa to British merchants.[26] While trade and even foreign company establishment in Taiwan was encouraged, missionaries and chapels and mission construction were not, particularly Christian ones.[27] Due to

---

[25] Wang, I-Shou. "Cultural Contact and the Migration of Taiwan's Aborigines", p. 40-42.

[26] Davidson, J. W. *The island of Formosa*. p. 206.

[27] Ibid., p. 205-206.

Formosan trade revitalization, the Japanese sent expeditions to Taiwan to re-engage trade negotiations with the Chinese and Europeans.[28] Taiwan became popular again as it had been during the Dutch and early Chinese periods, but that also meant the return of pirates and natives who raided and looted incoming ships and beached vessels unprotected by port defenses.[29] Although prosperous, the 1870s marked the beginning of the end for the lengthy Qing rule over Formosa.

The 19th century saw the arrival of French expeditions into Asia, particularly South-East Asia, as other European countries colonized countries in the Pacific Asia region. The French sought to expand their empires and scouted for lands from which to profit. The natural resources and territory of Southeast Asia appealed to the French, but the Chinese had already partly invested in these areas. The French saw the Chinese as an obstacle to their claims, so they invaded Vietnam, Laos, Cambodia, Taiwan, and parts of China in an attempt to stake their claim in Chinese ports.

While the French conquered the renamed French Indochina, now Vietnam, Laos, and Cambodia, they failed to establish permanent positions in either China or Taiwan. The Chinese on Formosa and along the coasts of China repelled the French assaults but exhausted valuable resources and men in the process. As a result, Taiwan, while able to slightly replenish itself, remained vul-

[28] Ibid., p. 208.

[29] Ibid., p. 215.

nerable to being defeated by and forced to secede to the Japanese within a decade.[30]

[30] Ibid., p. 220.

Chapter 2:

Industrialization of Japan

Commodore Matthew Perry arrived in Japan in 1853. Over the course of the next few years, Perry, with many U.S. commissioners and consuls, set up treaties with the Japanese government to open their ports and allow foreign trade, particularly with Western nations, including the U.S., the Netherlands, and Russia. On July 29, 1858, the Treaty of Amity and Commerce was proposed to allow U.S. ships and merchants to enter Japanese ports freely and, in return, the U.S. would protect Japanese naval expeditions. American diplomats and the Japanese government would settle ports in which the Americans would be allowed to control. As a result of this treaty, the Japanese relinquished power to dictate municipal and harbor regulations to the Americans.

The Tariffs Convention of 1866 would be one of the most significant treaties regarding the Japanese government's power, particularly concerning its foreign policies. All goods imported into Japan and transported by Japanese to areas within its empire would not have to pay taxes. Furthermore, both foreign and Japanese would be allowed to make payments with one another freely using their respective currency. The Japanese coin value dropped due to the increased use of foreign coins in Japan, as European merchandise entered the Japanese market at high prices.

The convention also affected the Japanese court system. Any American accused of misconduct against the Japanese would be tried and punished by American courts under American law. Japanese committing crimes against Americans, would be tried and punished by Japanese courts under Japanese law. While this appears fair, the U.S. had established a court system in Japanese harbors, but the Japanese did not have a similar court system. The convention allowed Americans more freedom in Japanese ports by allowing them to travel freely within 20 miles of the ports. The agreement also established trade regulations in which the Japanese had little control without permission from foreign nations.[31] In all, while the and other Western nations had more freedom over Japanese services, the Japanese government had more trading restrictions and foreign regulations as a result of the convention.

Policy changes from treaties issued in the Tariffs Convention of 1866, most prominently between the U.S. and Japan, led to the Meiji Restoration of 1868 and desire to remove and replace the shogun and daimyos from the feudal Japanese government. Food production shortages and rising famine related to Japan's isolation and

---

[31] Makoto, Matsuyama. "Japan and the Western Powers." *The North American Review* 127, no. 265 (1878): 406-26. www.jstor.org/stable/25100693, p. 406-409.

lack of natural resources led to the Meiji revolution. Due to the prohibition on imports and exports, materials, including food, had to be domestically produced, but low resources led to slow rates of production and cultivation. Once the Western treaties and tariffs opened Japan's doors, despite how unfair the provisions seemed, the Japanese realized the importance of foreign negotiations and open trade policies.

There was a need to reform Japan's political and social systems. Shoguns and daimyos led the feudal government while the emperor and imperial family served only as a religious entity and figurehead with few political contributions, which mostly came through the guidance of advisors. When the feudal government was overthrown, the emperor became head of the government with parliament houses and cabinet members acting as advisors, adopted from Western government systems. This change represented a blend of religious devotion to the imperial family, particularly the emperor, and political nationalism. With the emperor as leader, there would be a religious devotion to the head of the state. The two parliament houses contained the House of Peers, whose members were imperial family members and nobles; and the House of Commons, whose members were elected by the public. Voting privileges were granted to 25-year old males who lived in their district for more than a year and paid direct national taxes.

The political and social order changes also altered the understanding of nationalism in Japan. The new government gave way to divisions of Japanese people and their cultural views. One group could be considered traditionalists. They supported an isolationist state and the feudal government, and wanted to return to the customs and systems of ancient Japan. Their nationalism backed Japan's cultural, social, and political practices before the restoration.

Two other groups supported the new government and the new system, but in different ways. One group developed an inspiration to build a relationship with Western nations, primarily the U.S., and adopt similar institutions and culture. They felt that it would be necessary to trade and interact with Western governments to increase Japanese industrial and economic growth. Their belief centered around improving Japan by using other countries to help import and export goods and adapt particular Western culture to fit their needs. In essence, they believed relations between Japan and foreign nations would help improve Japan.

While the third group also endorsed adopting Western institutions and lifestyles, they also felt that Japan was strong enough to do this without needing to negotiate with Western countries. This group maintained confidence in Japan's capabilities to improve and provide the materials based on Western techniques to improve Japan's industrial and economic growth without support from other countries.[32]

---

[32] Moses, Bernard. "The Economic Situation in Japan." *Journal of Political Economy* 6, no. 2 (1898): 168-86. www.jstor.org/stable/1820363, p. 170-174.

Japan's ability to adopt, adapt, and utilize Western materials and applications led to rapid industrial growth in Japan, particularly in technology. The newly established government had more functions needing aid and promoting modern industries and institutions. Japan was able to rapidly develop its economy and industry independent of a foreign power, relying heavily on its mining and building upon its natural resources—particularly an abundant supply of copper, gold, coal, and iron. In 1884, Japan discovered more than 400 iron mines and collected over 11,000 tons of metal. For copper, over 500 mines were found and 10,500 tons collected. Coal production increased 800,000 tons by 1885. That same year, Japan gathered almost 1.2-million-yen worth of silk, which was domestically manufactured into clothing.

The industrial revolution and economic and industrial boom ended with Japan successfully producing more than 5-million-yen worth of pure and mixed goods. Under a national education system, 30,000 schools with a nationalized curriculum were built, which assisted in technological and advanced scientific studies to progress the development of Japan. Modern industries introduced new types of machinery to Japan, which speeded the industrial growth and advancement processes. From December 1886 to September 1887, 13 railroad companies were authorized and established, which ultimately constructed thousands of miles of railroads across Japan. In 1877, Japanese products began to compete in foreign markets with Chinese and Western manufacturers. Japan established 33 spinning factories, each producing 60,000 spindles of fabric.

Japan's industrial growth also caused urban population growth. Tokyo's population increased from approximately 800,000 to over a million. Osaka's population grew from approximately 290,000 to 360,000 residents. Kyoto's population increased from 13,000 to 80,000. By the end of 1886, of Japan's 38 million citizens, 3.5 million lived in cities, which grew from 20,000 before the industrial revolution. The advancements of industry and production enabled Japan to spread its imperial conquest over foreign competitors such as China and Russia at the turn of the 20th century. Japan's victory over China proved the capability and superiority of modern and Western implementations.

Despite Japan's rapid economic and industrial growth, improvement, and profit from natural resources, its materials remained limited to properly compete with foreign nations, creating a disadvantage when it came to rate of production.[33] The need for more resources, materials, and labor force incentivized the desire for imperialism and expansionism, which was being conducted by Western nations. The end of the 19th century made way for Japan to launch expansive campaigns, most notably towards Manchuria, Korea, and Taiwan.

On April 17, 1895, the Chinese signed the Treaty of Shimonoseki, following the disastrous defeat by the Japanese in the First Sino-Japanese War. This treaty marked

[33] Ibid., p. 184.

the end of the war and ceded many Chinese-owned islands to the Japanese, including Taiwan and the Pescadores Islands chain. While the agreement gave Taiwan to the Japanese, the Japanese did not take over Taiwan. Taiwan declared itself an independent republic with a governor and constitution. Realizing Taiwan could be of economic and strategic importance, Japan invaded Taiwan and conquered Taiwan by the end of 1895, but continued to struggle with guerrilla resistance until the end of the century.[34]

By the 1900s to 1910s, Taiwan had become Japan's most important trading center. During the first few years of its occupation, Japan's imports and exports from Taiwan exceeded 7.8-million-yen worth. Within ten years, by the early 1900s, that worth climbed to over 37 million yen. The primary exported goods were tea, rice, camphor oil, and coal. Valued imported goods included opium, kerosene oil, cotton, and timber. From both imported and exported goods, the Japanese in Taiwan secured four significant monopolies based on these goods. The monopolies of Taiwan included opium, camphor, tobacco, and salt.

Before Japanese occupation, a mass addiction to opium developed among the Taiwanese population, creating a massive market for opium imports. When the Japanese occupied Taiwan, they took over and created a monopoly for the opium industry. However, instead of expanding on the monopoly, the Japanese attempted to

---

[34] Grajdanzev, A. J. "Formosa (Taiwan) Under Japanese Rule." *Pacific Affairs* 15, no. 3 (1942): 31-124. doi:10.2307/2752241, p. 311-312.

increase public health and lessen widespread opium addiction. By controlling the opium business and regulating distribution, the Japanese hoped to discourage opium use and decrease the number of opium users. The only pre-Japanese occupation monopoly was salt. When the Japanese assumed control of the salt monopoly industry, they expanded the salt manufacturing rate and amount by growing the salt farms from 1700 acres to 60,000 acres. The salt would be provided to financially support Japan.

The tobacco industry was Taiwan's only monopoly to be greatly expanded, despite being inferior to foreign-grown tobacco. The most popular monopoly was the camphor industry due to its high demand for medicinal purposes. The Japanese government preserved the camphor forest and built more camphor factories, providing Japan with 1.5 million yen annually.[35]

Taiwan became essential to Japan as an economic and agricultural, supplying Japan with food sources, metals, and other resources not domestically available. As Taiwan used its resources to help supply Japan, Japan helped industrialize Taiwan to increase production rates, which increased supply rates to Japan.

Taiwan's development was built on agricultural production rates, modernization, and industrialization of Taiwan, along with population growth. Taiwan's manufacturing was influenced by imported industrial prod-

---

[35] Mackay, George W. "Japanese Administration in Formosa." *The Journal of Race Development* 2, no. 2 (1911): 172-87. doi:10.2307/29737905, p. 178-180.

ucts and the construction of modern industries and factories. Taiwan's agricultural and industrial development were essential investments for both Taiwan and Japan because the industrialization of Taiwan and construction of modern industrial factories improved the agrarian production rate, mining of valuable natural materials, such as metals, and increased travel time between ports in Taiwan which increased export and import rates. The industrial growth helped develop and industrialize Taiwan to such an increased rate that by 1933, 7,000 factories were constructed. The growth rate of the sugar industry, the most crucial supply to Japan, increased 6% annually from 1912 to 1940.

The sugar industry in Taiwan became so crucial to Japan that in the 1920s, sugar accounted for 60% of Taiwan's industries; in the 1930s, it dropped to 50%. In the first half of the 1910s, the sugar production rate increased 88%.[36]

Alongside the sugar industry, rice emerged as an essential export to Japan. Colonial Taiwan's economy relied heavily on rice and sugar exports to Japan. Ninety percent of both sugar and rice production was exported to Japan. Food exports made up 84% of the total output exported to Japan, most of which involved rice and sugar. The export numbers showed the importance of Taiwan's agriculture for Japan's economic growth.[37] During the 1930s, focus

---

[36] Samuel P. S. Ho. "The Economic Development of Colonial Taiwan: Evidence and Interpretation." *The Journal of Asian Studies* 34, no. 2 (1975): 417 39. doi:10.2307/2052756, p. 421-422.

[37] Ibid., p. 427-428.

shifted from building on food sources to mining and establishing modernized industries for metals and chemicals to prepare Japan for military campaigns.

To aid and accelerate goods transported across Taiwan and trade growth with Japan, the Japanese worked on improving and expanding Taiwan's railroads, roads, and ports. The two largest harbors in Taiwan, Keelung in the north and Kaohsiung in the south, were connected by a single railway to improve the movement of goods from one side of the country to the other.[38] Since the occupation of Taiwan, Japan established favorable sea lines that allowed ships' passageway between Japan, China, and Taiwan. The ports of Keelung and Nagasaki allowed steamers carrying more than 6,000 tons, while Chinese ports required smaller and slower vessels. The Keelung harbor was the superior Taiwan harbor because of its capability to provide for large steamers.

Within Taiwan, Japan built over 6,000 miles of roads. While their methods improved transportation and allowed for faster travel between ports by cutting across the island, roads ran through farms and many properties owned by Taiwanese peasants. Peasants lost significant portions of their land, particularly those of small farmers.[39]

Taiwan's economic growth resulted in export growth. Japanese influence on Taiwan's agricultural and industrial development allowed for an increase in the production rate, which increased exports to Japan. Exports tripled from 1900 to 1910, increasing six fold by the end of

[38] Ibid., p. 422.

[39] Mackay, George W. "Japanese Administration in Formosa," p. 180-181.

the 1930s. Ninety percent of the shares of Taiwan's exports were sent to Japan. The value of exports also accelerated. By the end of the 1930s, the total amount of Taiwan's exports exceeded 320 million yen's worth from 25 million at the beginning of the century.[40] The Japanese successfully produced and gained significant materials and profit from their colony in Taiwan. Through the modernization and industrialization, the industrial and agricultural growth of Taiwan also affected the growth and benefits for Japan.

Along with leveraging Taiwan as an economic and agricultural resource, assimilating the native Taiwanese population was another fundamental goal for the Japanese. The Japanese saw Taiwan as a tool to assist the Japanese Empire in becoming self-sufficient without reliance on foreign trade. This goal and purpose would affect treatment of the natives and other inhabitants, along with usage of the land, particularly acreage belonging to peasants. The modernization of society and assimilation of the native population would lead to the native population being able to work with modernized industries.

Assimilating colonial Taiwan primarily involved promoting Japanese education. The Japanese administration encouraged Taiwanese natives to enter educational institutions, which prompted the teaching of modern science and techniques. Taiwan's Japanese Governor-General, Kodama Gentaro, and principal Japanese educator in Taiwan, Isawa Shuji, introduced schools from primary to

---

[40] Samuel P. S. Ho. "The Economic Development of Colonial Taiwan," p. 426-428.

higher education, including medical education, to educate Taiwanese natives on Japanese language, culture, with an emphasis on math and science. To use Taiwan as a valued resource, the Japanese not only exploited Taiwan's natural labor, they also used natives as laborers to support the use of modern industries and productivity of Taiwan's materials. The Japanese encouraged natives to provide labor by promoting specific fields of education, particularly in medical, economic, and agricultural areas. This promotion pushed the natives to work in these fields, increasing food and industrial production rates for Japan.

The government movement increased the native school-aged population attending schools from 300 to 2400 from 1915 to 1922. Japanese education promoted native loyalty towards the ambition and position of the Japanese, along with Japanese values and culture. Japanese values and culture had more influence on the urban population.[41]

Taiwanese males, through the influence of the education system, were guided to specialize in economic and agricultural fields, which increased the number of agricultural and industrial laborers contributing to growing product production rates. Native laborers were used to fulfill the Japanese goal of making Taiwan a market for Japanese products and supporting Japan's industrial and economic growth. Males in industrial jobs expanded to

---

[41] Tsurumi, E. Patricia. "Education and Assimilation in Taiwan under Japanese Rule, 1895-1945." *Modern Asian Studies* 13, no. 4 (1979): 617-41. www.jstor.org/stable/312185, p. 618-628.

over 130,000 from approximately 80,000 in nearly a quarter of a century. Until the late 1930s, agricultural jobs made up 69% of the male working population. Male agricultural jobs declined to 61% by 1940 due to the significant shift to industrial labor, the majority of which went to manufacturing and trading industries. The manufacturing industry drove the need for rapid industrial production rates to support Japan's upcoming military campaign against the U.S.; the trading industry helped export industrial products.[42]

To maintain political, economic, and social control to direct the population and benefit them, the Japanese established a colonial administration with policies that, while successful in monitoring and increasing Taiwan's and Japan's economic and industrial growth, pressured and discriminated against Taiwanese inhabitants, leading to several armed resistances early in the occupation. Japanese authorities used a "hoko" system that tracked registrations for community members usually in ten households, as well as the city leader. While the system under colonial authorities enforced, to a degree, laws and managed Taiwanese communities, Japanese police treatment of inhabitants and because Japanese cities lacked such strict housing enforcement policies, these issues ultimately led to armed Taiwanese resistance.

The Japanese also applied another form of household policy revolving around censuses and household registration. For this system, Japanese colonial authorities

[42] Samuel P. S. Ho. "The Economic Development of Colonial Taiwan," p. 423-425.

documented the births, deaths, and marriages of each household member. Literate household members recorded and reported actions and events directed by community leaders.

The strict control over the communities resulted from a strong police presence, in addition to the strict Japanese policies. The number of police, most of whom were Japanese, increased from one officer for roughly two thousand natives, to one for approximately five hundred natives. The Japanese also directed one native for every three police to assist in controlling communities of eight hundred households. While the police force seemed to increase, they remained spread thin in controlling the native mass population; however, they were strict and demanding on the people, which served as another factor that motivated an armed resistance.

Japanese economic policies aimed to exploit natives and mountain resources, modernize the sugar industry, and increase taxes. Taxes on natives were made more burdensome via heavy policing on tax evasion and the strict tax collection.[43] The unequal treatment of the Taiwanese compared with the less strict policies on Japanese contributed to the rise of native resistance.

Taiwanese and Chinese elites caused the rapid mobilization of the resistance movement. In 1915, in the sub province of Ta-pa-ni, Taiwanese-Chinese and Taiwanese

---

[43] Katz, Paul R. "Governmentality and Its Consequences in Colonial Taiwan: A Case Study of the Ta-pa-ni Incident of 1915." *The Journal of Asian Studies* 64, no. 2 (2005): 387-424. www.jstor.org/stable/25075755, p. 398-399.

natives revolted against Japanese police and civil and military officials. Initially, local Ta-pa-ni elites in villages had to recruit members to support their cause by forming an organization based on rituals and a true belief. They created banners, performed rituals, ate a vegetarian diet, and protested against the Japanese and colonialism in general. Members were required to enter through initiation rituals and wore unique jewels to symbolize their membership. As another practice, members captured Japanese civil and military officials, as well as civilians, and executed them as human sacrifices.

The protest movement also sent armed militias after the police and army forces in the region. In response, from July to December 1915, the Japanese reinforced with more police and military personnel to put down the resistance. The Ta-pa-ni Incident cost the lives of more than 1,700 villagers, both revolt participants and innocents deemed as potential threats. The Ta-pa-ni Incident led to anti-insurgent operations against natives from the mountains to prevent future resistance.[44]

Even following attempts to put down resistance movements, sporadic uprisings and some organized revolts continued to exist. To expedite the assimilation process, the Japanese suppressed or extinguished local customs or traditions. Japanese police stationed at local villages were used to impose forced assimilation.

However, the village tribesmen of Wushe refused to relinquish their tribal customs. Following a dispute between

---

[44] Ibid., p. 402-408, 412-413.

Japanese police and officials, and Wushe tribesmen regarding the local tribal marriage ceremonies (which the Japanese perceived as threatening), tribesmen retaliated by assaulting local elites loyal to the Japanese. After the assault that killed over 100 Japanese and injured another 200, the Japanese governor of Taiwan sent police and military to put down the offenders. Within 50 days of the uprising, a Japanese force of almost 4,000 police, soldiers, and mercenaries killed over 900 natives.[45]

While the first few decades of Japanese occupation encountered sporadic tribal resistance, the 1920s gave rise to a more organized anti-Japanese, anti-Colonial political movement. Political activist movement members were mostly middle and high-class Taiwanese. In 1920, conservative political activist leaders were the first to establish political anti-colonial movements with clear demands. They protested against Taiwanese discrimination in household policies and demanded change to make the systems more equal for both Japanese and Taiwanese. They also started a petition campaign to establish a local parliament within Japan's national Diet, or legislation. The Japanese tried to suppress the resistance through threats, arrests, and police harassment, but, the signatures continued to increase regardless. In 1925, petition signatures totaled approximately 800, expanding to roughly 2,500 within two years. As a result of rising support for policy reforms, in 1921 initial petitioners founded the Taiwan Cultural Association, an organiza-

[45] "The Wushe Incident—Taiwan Today." Accessed January 3, 2020. https://taiwantoday.tw/news.php?post=25171&unit=20,29,35,45.

tion criticizing Japan's colonial government and discussing changes to make policies more equal to Taiwanese.

The Associations wanted to spread reformist ideas through public lectures that criticized discrimination within Japanese policies and treatment of Taiwanese. Left-wing association members and political activists condemned conservatives for arguing to join the Japanese government and gaining a seat in Japan's parliament, viewing this as opposed to resisting Japanese occupation and colonial rule. As a result of political disagreements, conservative members left the association to form the Taiwan Popular Party, which protested discriminatory policies against Taiwanese.[46]

Many left-wing activists were Taiwanese students attracted to the ideas of anarchism and communism while studying abroad in Japan and China. Through their experiences abroad, particularly in China, the students developed a radical anti-imperialist view. They formed organizations with Koreans to build ideas to overthrow Japanese imperialism in their home nation. Upon returning to Taiwan, the Taiwanese students not only heavily opposed Japanese colonial authority, they also opposed natives conservatives for their moderate stance and desire to participate in Japanese lawmaking. Leftist students were critical of the petition movement and lectures led by the Taiwan Cultural Association, and often actively voiced their disdain.

---

[46] Tsurumi, E. Patricia. "Education and Assimilation in Taiwan," p. 630-633.

While both left-wing and conservative political activists opposed each other's goals on the Japanese rule, they united on issues involving farmers. Both political sides desired to tackle threats and pressure on farmers from agricultural corporations and the Japanese colonial government. Yet, even with a common issue, the approach differed. The goal of the conservatives was to raise awareness of a Taiwanese national identity for the farmers; left-leaning political activists devoted their efforts to forming unions and campaigns with farmers to engage the Japanese.[47] Taiwanese political activists, while having different agendas and actions, succeeded in establishing and reinforcing a Taiwanese national identity.

Despite the political activist and protest movement, Japan maintained control over the native community in Taiwan. Japan also continued to leverage Taiwan as an economic, agricultural, and industrial resource. In 1945, the Japanese were finally forced to leave Taiwan as a result of their World War II loss to the U.S.

[47] Ibid., p. 637-640.

Chapter 3:

China During WWII

While the Taiwanese laid a national identity foundation, so did the Chinese. The Kuomintang (KMT) movement, formed and led by Sun Yat-sen, comparable to a Western movement. The KMT concept and its leaders had many Western qualities from being educated in Western countries and followers of Christianity. The Communist Party, introduced in 1920, emerged as a primary concern and focus of Chiang Kai-shek's efforts. Before Japan's invasion, Chiang Kai-shek spent over a billion Chinese yuan in six military expeditions against the Communist Party. The communists, while not politically or militarily superior, consistently fended off KMT assaults and opposed the KMT Government's imposition and rule over the peasants.[48]

Japan's interests in China formed around an increasing need for alternative and expanding need for resources. Japan wanted to modernize China, as it had with Taiwan, and planned to manipulate and industrial-

---

[48] Sokolsky, George E. "Political Movements in China." *The Annals of the American Academy of Political and Social Science* 168 (1933): 18-22. www.jstor.org/stable/1019031, p. 20-22.

ize and advance China's production rates. In particular, China's rice industry would benefit Japan's industrial and economic growth.

China's mineral wealth was another essential appeal to Japan's imperialist goals. Japan wanted to survey and take advantage of its coal, iron, and ore. As an essential asset to Japan's interests, Manchuria, bordering China and the Soviet Union, was vital for Japan's occupation as it guarded against any possible assistance the Chinese might receive from the Soviet Union.[49] Though many journalists during the 1930s believed that Japan would use China solely for economic and industrial resources, Japan's anti-Chinese superiority complex but also resulted in the oppression and attempted extermination of the Chinese population.

Upon establishing a government in China and signing a treaty establishing anti-communist and Chinese-Japanese collaborative ideas, the Japanese government used the plans to form new policies for its Chinese puppet government. The new policies were proposed to put an end to attempts to resist the Japanese and have China as a strategic position for Japan as well as means to gain material resources for the support in the fight against the Western nations. Japan also wanted to use its newly established puppet government to aid its efforts against communism in China and prevent its spread throughout Asia, as it represented a threat to their goal for the Greater East Asia Co-Prosperity Sphere.

---

[49] "Japan and China." *World Affairs* 100, no. 3 (1937): 136-34. www.jstor.org/stable/20662942, p. 137-138.

Japan's Greater East Asia Co-Prosperity Sphere was the concept that Japan would unite all of Asia under the control of its new policies and influences. Under these new policies, Japan would gain the capabilities to utilize the conquered territories' economic and material wealth and oppress native populations.

In China, the head of the puppet government was Wang Ching-wei, a former Kuomintang leader and compatriot of Sun Yat-sen. Wang, under Japanese support and supervision, built his regime on policies designed by the Japanese and formed a centralized government based in the Chinese capital of Nanjing as mandated by the Japanese government in Tokyo.[50] China was not only used to provide Japan with supplies, Japan also exerted influence over China's population. It became a practical ground for Japan to test plans to change China's political, social, economic, and industrial structure to benefit Japan's growth. China served as an important test subject due to its more centrally structured society, and Japan wanted to test Western nations' reactions to this exploitation before hitting Western colonies located in the Pacific.

With Japan's technological and military superiority to China, and with little initial aid from the Western nations, both the Nationalist Government and the Communist Party were forced to fight on a separate and more sporadic front. 1935 seemed to be the worst year in Chinese history, prior to 1937, due to Japanese military mo-

---

[50] Johnstone, William C. "Japan's "New" China Policy." *Far Eastern Survey* 12, no. 19 (1943): 185-91. doi:10.2307/3023282, p. 185-188.

bilization against the Nationalist Government and the Chinese political and military failures leading to the forced dismantling of the centralized Nationalist Government. Japan launched assaults in the summer of 1935. Five provinces in North China, including three Manchurian areas and two southern areas of the Great Wall, fell to overwhelming Japanese forces within days. Local generals in these regions were not under a central command nor had an organized or superior strength; therefore, they were easily defeated. The Nationalist Government under Chiang Kai-shek failed to supply northern armies with support, nor planned any sign of resistance as the government tried to appease the Japanese and desist their aggressive movements against the Chinese.

Anti-Japanese meetings, demonstrations, and any anti-Japanese sentiments in public news were prohibited or censored to reinforce cooperation between China and Japan. Only after Nationalist Party members and the Kuomintang Congress had yielded to Japan's demand to be disbanded and submit to the Japanese did Chiang finally actively send armies into forwarding areas in China with determination to establish concentrated resistance. The Japanese saw a rise in hostile attitude from Chiang and the Chinese military, leading to the viewing him as a threat to Japan's plan to reorganize and reconstruct China. Through 1935, Chiang hoped to use diplomatic tactics to work with Japan, so he did not publicly express strong anti-Japanese sentiments.

In 1936, Chiang strengthened his anti-Japanese feelings following increased Japanese military actions and the dismantling of the Kuomintang Congress and Nationalist Party. He ultimately announced his determination to combat the Japanese military and lead Chinese military forces against them. By December 1936, Chiang had gained the support of the Chinese population and was widely viewed as the national leader of China.[51]

During the same time, the Japanese Government assigned Ambassador Shigeru Kawagoe to China to open negotiations. Even though both China and Japan had become militarily engaged, diplomatic discussions and negotiations between the two countries continued in an attempt to reach peaceful alternatives. Kawagoe started with a list of demands requested of China. These demands included allowing a commercial airline between China and Japan, cooperating in controlling Korean revolutionaries and anti-Japanese activities, and hiring Japanese advisers. The claims and counterclaims discussed between China and Japan became the foundation for their new relationship. Negotiations and diplomacy addressed and assessed the relations and demands between Chinese and Japanese authorities. China agreed to reform its tariffs by putting pressure on smugglers and accepting Japanese advisers.

Despite intentions from the Chinese to cooperate and negotiate with Japan, Chiang Kai-shek and the Chinese population had grown stronger in their determination to

---

[51] Yutang, Lin. "China Prepares to Resist." *Foreign Affairs* 15, no. 3 (1937): 472-83. Accessed January 7, 2020. doi:10.2307/20028786, p. 472-477.

endure and withstand the Japanese military. First, Japan's constant acts of aggression slowly unified and reinforced the national identity and goals of the Chinese population. The Chinese national force strengthened and became more organized due to the rising anti-Japanese attitude and a passionate hatred towards the Japanese. These feelings under a strong leader led to a surge of self-confidence in China's own strength and capability.

A second reason for China's rise in aggressiveness was the population's newfound confidence in their abilities and their leader, Chiang Kai-shek. Upon becoming China's national leader, Chiang grew more determined and prepared to fight the Japanese when needed, yet he continued open negotiations as a possible means of avoiding violence. Chiang knew that, at this time, the Japanese had advantages over Chiang's military force and would therefore have to wait and prepare until able to match the Japanese. Chiang understood the importance of winning centered on supplying his armies, having trained soldiers and an air force, possessing ample military power by recruiting civilians, having adequate funding for these needs, and devising detailed strategies to best combat superior Japanese forces. Due to the trust and confidence that the Chinese people had in Chiang, he was able to encourage and persuade college men and women to join the military and nursing services, respectively, and to mobilize a robust mechanized army.

The third point that inspired China's determined resistant and aggressive nature against the Japanese was Russia's possible intervention. If Russia allied itself with

China and entered into war with Japan to support China, Japan would be forced to match both China and Russia's much more substantial and technologically superior combined military force.[52]

China's war with Japan involved not only the Nationalist Government and Japan, but also the Communist Party, which fled to the hills in the late 1920s after being dislodged by the Nationalist Army. The war with Japan shaped the socio-political issues of both the Nationalist Government and the Communist Party, eventually leading back into civil war and the post-Cold War China. The Nationalist and Communist Parties originated from the social and political change and modernization of China that was desired to overthrow the imperial system. The Nationalist Party emerged as a state-party with a close societal relationship when dealing with China's socio-economic issues. While the Nationalist Party became corrupt and ineffective, its original objective should be understood as a positive and well-intentioned goal to replace the former socio-political system.

Two Nationalist Party approaches employed to address the formation of an emerging socio-political structure were using culture as a means of propaganda and advancing a collective responsibility for the underprivileged. The Nationalist Government-issued social policies that targeted issues such as aiding the impoverished, accepting and assisting refugees, and modifying the form of citizenship.

---

[52] Ibid., p. 478-483.

Before the 1940s, the Nationalist Government also had a positive effect on China's economy. China had an abundance of harvest linked to the satisfying provision of food and low costs. Unfortunately, despite the initial prosperous period, the Japanese campaigns and pressure on the Nationalist Government led to the decline of the economy. China, during the late-war period, faced hyperinflation and a corresponding rise in black markets and corruption. The Nationalist Government was unproductive in managing its economy. The lack of controlled currency eventually led to inflation and a high price increases.

Wartime China showed the economic and political changes of the Nationalist Government and the rise of influence and power in the Communist Party, particularly the growth of its impact on peasants. Communist views for supplying societal welfare and mass mobilization seemed to directly contrast the Nationalist's policies.[53] The 1940s, at the height of war, displayed the strengths of the Communist Party and the influence it developed with people as trust and confidence in the Nationalist Government declined.

During the war, the Communists established anti-Japanese sites in Northern and Central China around their capital in the city of Yenan. They conducted guerilla and defensive tactics against the Japanese. While the

---

[53] Mitter, Rana, and Aaron William Moore. "China in World War II, 1937-1945: Experience, Memory, and Legacy." *Modern Asian Studies* 45, no. 2 (2011): 225-40. Accessed January 10, 2020. www.jstor.org/stable/25835677, p. 229-231.

Communists had similar military size as the Nationalists, yet technologically and materially inferior, they gained morale from the popularity and control of civilians, particularly the peasant population. The Communists influenced and rallied 95 million civilians against the Japanese more effectively than their Nationalist counterparts.[54] The Communists, to combat the Japanese imperialists and Nationalist Government devised a theory based on Mao's work, "On New Democracy," aimed to construct a new state with new politics, economy, and culture. Mao's "New Democracy" was both a theory and a bourgeoisie-democratic revolution. Mao called for the proletariat and bourgeoisie union against imperialists and bureaucrats. The "New Democracy" theorized a state system based on a joint dictatorship over all classes, led by the proletariat.[55]

The principles and policies of the "New Democracy" were managed and utilized by the members of the United Front, a popular political group holding local offices in various Chinese regions, a third of which were communists. Most of these officials resided in the Yenan region and other communist-controlled areas. The "New Democracy" advanced the economic and social growth of the people, extending their influence and gaining more supporters. Meetings held by the representatives

---

[54] Stein, Gunther. "The Other China." *Foreign Affairs* 24, no. 1 (1945): 62-74. Accessed January 11, 2020. doi:10.2307/20029945, p. 62-63.
[55] "On New Democracy." Accessed January 11, 2020. https://www.marxists.org/reference/archive/mao/selected-works/volume-2/mswv2_26.htm.

focused on administrative policies and ideas for villages, regions, and the entire country. The cooperation between local representatives and communists led to the growth of United Front membership and increased support for applying the policies of the "New Democracy." Through the support it gained from influencing regions under the United Front, the Communist military gained more supplies, recruits, and training, and grew to more than a million troops, mostly peasants and rural people from the Yenan region. Yenan representatives of the United Front implemented policies and principles in their areas. Their goal was to analyze and understand the economic and social progress from systems of the "New Democracy."

The "New Democracy" economic and financial policies allowed for improved living standards and increased production. The Communists were able to solve many economic issues plaguing the Nationalist Government, including land tenure reformation. The new reforms reduced tenants' rents to approximately 40 percent of their initial land, leaving roughly 60 percent under local government control, Tenants were paid for the 60 percent that they had relinquished.

Next, farmers were told to pool their labor and resources with other farmers and work on collective lands, as opposed to individual property. Some farmers would also contribute to working on industrial production. This new strategy increased agricultural and industrial production rates.

Finally, taxes were lowered, and lower fees sent to Communist military forces demanded as government officials were provided a satisfying lifestyle while remaining beholden to the will of the people. The lowered taxes and fees allowed all citizens, including political officials, soldiers, students, and teachers, to participate in agricultural and industrial work, which contributed to rising production.

The social and cultural policies of the "New Democracy" were also reformed and had effective results. The public health and education systems were improved significantly and successfully—the new educational system allowed education to be available for citizens of all ages and educational backgrounds. The Communists also organized mass movements influenced by cultural programs and arts and encouraged by "New Democracy" principles. Support and passion for the Communist Party rose due to its policies and victories against the Japanese. Meanwhile, support for the Nationalists slowly declined.

Another advantage the Communists had over the Nationalist Government was greater integration and involvement with the military, which led to an improved war effort contribution, easier military mobilization, and organized civilian and military cooperation. Of the 95 million communists, 16 million joined the Self Defense Corps and were expertly trained for a variety of services and operations. Two million troops were trained as elite members and seen as more combat ready. From these militia groups, highly-trained troops were redeployed into the Communist regular army. At the start of the war, the Communists' Eighth Route Army and the New Fourth Army had a combined force of 95,000 men. By the end of the war, the new combined strength increased to approximately 900,000. The Communists were effective in overt and covert, offensive and defensive anti-Japanese operations. They engaged in guerilla tactics to obstruct Japanese communication and supply lines, and to pin down major Japanese forces in strategically chosen defensive locations to prevent them from striking more essential targets. Due to their practical actions, Communists became a more significant threat to the Japanese than the Nationalists.

Compared to the Nationalists, the Communist forces caused considerably more damage and frequently outmaneuvered the Japanese more successfully. The Communists also had exceptional population support and war efforts supplying resources to their troops. While the Communists and Nationalists worked independently of each other, the United States, which had been supplying the Nationalist government with arms and military advisers, wanted to merge the Communists and Nationalists to prevent another civil war after Japan's defeat.[56]

Chiang Kai-shek desperately needed American assistance, but the U.S. wanted to encourage unity between the Nationalists and Communists. To promote their resolve after the war, the U.S. had to provide Chiang with enough military, economic, and moral support to defeat the Japanese, but not enough to fight the Com-

[56] Stein, Gunther. "The Other China," p. 66-71.

munists after the war.[57]

America's goal to provide support to China was because China's stability and struggle against the Japanese were outstanding. China had geological and geopolitical importance, as well as military, social, and cultural significance. For the U.S., China was strategically important because in continuing to resist, the Japanese would have devoted vast resources in maintaining control over China. The Japanese would lack the resources to fight the U.S., which had developed an idealized, positive view of China and the Nationalist Government, despite its corruption and incompetence. The U.S. supported the Chinese with arms, oil, gasoline, ships, vehicles, and aircraft, as well as experienced military advisers and pilots, which would provide air support for the Chinese to combat the Japanese.

While the U.S. continued to remain militarily, economically, and politically neutral in the war, it dispatched retired Air Corps Tactical School instructor and pilot Claire Chennault to China to be Chiang Kai-shek's acting advisor. In 1940 and 1941, Chennault was sent nearly 100 volunteer pilots and 200 ground crews along with 100 P-40s to form the American Volunteer Group, later known as the "Flying Tigers," which would engage with the Japanese Air Force and target Japanese military installations, supply convoys, and troop movements. From December 1941 to July 1942, the Flying Tigers downed almost 300 Japanese planes and cost the Japanese 1,500 men. In contrast, the Flying Tigers lost 12

[57] Ibid., p. 64.

airplanes and ten pilots in combat and another three pilots and 61 planes on the ground. The victories of Flying Tigers helped boost China's morale and stun Japanese movements.[58]

It was not only the Western nations and their Pacific Asian colonies, China, and Japan to be heavily impacted by the war in the Pacific. Along with the islands under U.S. invasion in their campaign against Japan, Taiwan, a Japanese colony and major economic and industrial resource, became a primary strategic bombing target for the Americans. Kay Chen, who lived on the Penghu Islands during the war, witnessed her hometown, Magong, bombed frequently by American planes. Kay's family had a private bunker next to her mother's temple, where attackers tried to avoid hitting, but many bombs hit near her home nevertheless.

During one incident, when the sirens sounded, Kay and her family ran into the bunker with one older woman who cried out, "I hope I don't have to see through World War III anymore!" Throughout Kay's experiences running into the bomb shelter, she always brought along the doll that her father bought when he returned from a trip to England. The widespread fear caused by the devastating bombing raids on Taiwanese civilians, including Kay and her family, led to hatred for Americans. As the war ended,

---

[58] "The United States and China During World War II: An..." Accessed January 15, 2020.
https://china.usembassy-china.org.cn/our-relationship/policy-history/io/shared-sacrifice-u-s-china-cooperation-world-war-ii/united-states-china-world-war-ii-operational-outline/.

radio stations began broadcasting that "Taipei was at peace," and there was no need to hide in bomb shelters.[59]

The cooperation and alliance between the U.S. and China became a decisive factor in the victory over Japan in a brief amount of time. The relationship between the two countries also affected their actions and motives going into the Cold War era. The U.S., as a significant ally and supporter of the Nationalist Government, looked for potential sanctuary bases for Nationalists who fled the overwhelming Communist forces, which had gained strength and public support following the war against the Japanese and the corrupt Nationalist Government. The U.S. and Nationalist Government decided on Taiwan as a prominent base for the Nationalists and anti-Communist Chinese.

With the backing of General Douglas MacArthur, Supreme Commander for the Allied Powers, and the U.S. military and government, in early October 1949 Nationalist Revolutionary leaders Chiang Kai-shek and Chen Chong established themselves and their supporters in Taiwan. MacArthur's advisors to Chiang Kai-shek recommended reformation within the Taiwanese Government. As a result, Chen Chong and Chinese political figure, K. C. Wu, became head of the military and civil administrations in Taiwan, respectively.[60]

---

[59] Chen, Kay. Interview by Ellen Hickman. Oral Interview. November 29, 2019.

[60] Central Intelligence Agency to Department of State, Report, October 25, 1949, CIA-RDP82-00457R003600190009-7, CREST System, General CIA Records.

Chapter 4:

Taiwan under KMT

Following Japan's surrender, the Nationalist Government retook control of Taiwan and used an initial refugee base for leaders of the Nationalist Government. Before the Nationalist movement to Taiwan, the U.S. had been assessing Taiwan through documented studies recorded by the CIA. The CIA aimed to research the political, geological, and military advantages of Taiwan to incite U.S. aid and funding incentives for Nationalists to move back to Taiwan. With a refugee base for Nationalist Government leaders being established on Taiwan, any support or chance of Nationalists remaining on the mainland dwindled as the new Nationalist Government refuge supplemented the ineffectiveness and defeatist attitude they displayed. By 1949, the Nationalist military had also gradually moved to Taiwan and established a military base there.

To the CIA and U.S. Government, Taiwan did not offer strategic supplies, yet could be used as an essential political, military, economic, and agricultural asset. A significant problem for the Nationalist Government developed from disagreements and conflicts within the party. The Nationalist Government had to be more centralized and concentrated. While Chiang Kai-shek remained as president, he appointed K. C. Wu as the Provincial Governor of Taiwan and Chen Chong as leader of the Nationalist military.

Wu's loyalty to Chiang and experience as mayor of Shanghai led to Chiang's trust for Wu in acting independently to reform the civil administration. Still, Wu's administrative power in Taiwan remained strictly limited to civilian control, as the Nationalist Government seemed to overrule Wu in all other issues. Due to its geographical location, Taiwan could provide air and naval bases to prevent communists from disrupting supplies running from the Philippines to Japan, while being equally supplied by Japan. The CIA also documented the Nationalist military strength in Taiwan to analyze its capabilities and limitations in preparation for a possible communist invasion of the island.

The Nationalist military consisted of a total of an estimated 420,000 military personnel. The military force included almost 300,000 Army, 80,000 Air Force, and 40,000 Navy personnel. The Army had 35 infantry divisions, including 23,000 Armored Forces staff and 6,000 under Artillery Command. The Navy had 17 operational combat ships, 21 being repaired and refitted, and 38 auxiliary and smaller ships. The Air Force's functional strength consisted of 174 fighters, 91 light bombers, 13 reconnaissance planes, and 198 transport. While Chen Chong led the military, it was Chiang who coordinated movements and structured the organization. Military effectiveness and ineffectiveness revolved around Chiang's leadership and his capabilities as he wanted personal control over the military.[61]

Taiwan had a substantial amount of exportable goods and increased agricultural production. Taiwan's food production proved valuable in supplementing China's and Japan's food-deficit economies. It's main food exports to Japan were rice and sugar. While having a smaller industrial sector than Japan due to the insignificant scale of the industrial sector in most Far East countries, Taiwan still had considerable size in comparison.[62]

Taiwan's economic and agricultural status was a significant reason to attract the U.S. interests and aid, as its harvest and agricultural surpluses led to an abundance of food supplies for the Nationalist Government. The rice crop in 1949 and 1948 remained essentially the same at 1.2 million tons per year. Due to Nationalist land reforms with aid from the U.S., agricultural production boosted during the 1950s. Another reason for the food surplus was the absence of need to provide food supplies for the mainland population, which allowed for greater amounts to be used in Taiwan's foreign trade. The food surplus relied on the accessibility of the fertilizers supplied by Taiwan's Economic Cooperation Agreement

---

[61] Central Intelligence Agency to Department of State, Report, February 27, 1950, CIA-RDP79-01143A000100100062-3, CREST System, General CIA Records, p. 3-5.

[62] Central Intelligence Agency to Department of State, National Intelligence Estimates, February 1, 1949, 0000258551, FOIA, National Intelligence Council Collection, p. 2.

(ECA), which provided fertilizers from foreign sources.[63]

The U.S. provided economic and military aid to the Taiwan Government via $1 billion in financial support, while U.S. military aid unburdened Taiwan's local resources for other uses. The U.S.'s economic contribution allowed the Taiwan Government to launch three Four-Year programs focused on developing and improving Taiwan's commercial, industrial, and agricultural growth. The first program, launched in 1953, received a 6.8 million investment from the Taiwan Government in New Taiwan dollars ("N.T."), equating to $272 million USD. The program resulted in a 22% increase in agricultural production, focusing on seed selection and fertilizer and sugar production. Industrial production, which focused on mining, manufacturing, transportation, communication, and electricity, grew by 55%, and the total GNP rose by 34%.

The second Four-Year plan started in 1957, with the Taiwan Government devoting 20 billion NT ($800 billion USD). It stressed the development of natural resources, export expansion, the trade balance of payment, and job opportunities. The plan caused the national income to increase by 30%, industrial and agricultural production rose by 57% and 20%, respectively. Exports and imports achieved a yearly average of $170 million and $252 million USD, respectively.

The third Four-Year Plan invested primarily in in-

---

[63] Central Intelligence Agency to Department of State, Report, February 27, 1950, CIA-RDP79-01143A000100100062-3, CREST System, General CIA Records, p. 9.

dustrial and agricultural production, along with exports and imports. Within the industrial sector, there was an emphasis on energy producing and heavy industries, such as plastic, glass, machinery, steel, and ship and car building. The plan increased GNP by 36%, industrial and agricultural productions by 57.6% and 23.2%, respectively, and exports and imports by $260 million and $320 million USD yearly, respectively.

For the first five years of Taiwan under the new Nationalist Government, the U.S. provided economic support to repair Taiwan's war damage. The latter half of the 1950s saw U.S. aid focus on the development of the transport, power, and manufacturing sectors. By 1960, the U.S. shifted its focus to the private sector, export-earning abilities, and self-sustaining economic capabilities. The U.S. provided Taiwan a total of $3.7 billion for financial and military aid. The U.S. Department of Defense devoted $2.3 billion of military support, while $1.4 billion went to Taiwan's economy.[64]

The Nationalist Government not only made economic and land reforms, it had to make political reforms due to corruption during the Japanese war, which caused their mainland downfall during the Chinese Civil War.

On January 5, 1949, Chen Cheng became the governor of Taiwan. By December, the Nationalist Government would become fully established in Taiwan and shift the governorship position to K. C. Wu. Nationalists assumed

---

[64] Chang, David W. "U.S. Aid and Economic Progress in Taiwan." Asian Survey 5, no. 3 (1965): 152-60. Accessed January 18, 2020. doi:10.2307/2642405, p. 152-155.

total control of the National Government of Taiwan upon their establishment, meaning they also controlled local political parties. The Nationalist Party analyzed the policies of the National Government to understand appropriate reform plans that would be efficient and effective.

The main branch of the National Government was the National Congress. The National Congress held meetings with the Central Executive Committee and Central Supervisory Committee, where policies were proposed and administered. Under the Reform Plan, the two committees were replaced by the Central Reform Committee, which had 16 members, and the Advisory Committee, which had 25 members. The Reform Committee consisted of men with an average age of 48 who regulated the plan. On the other hand, the Advisor Committee, consisting of men averaging age of 66, who supervised the government. The goal of the new Reform Plan was to centralize the government, abolish corruption, and recruit highly patriotic political members, who were mostly agricultural and industrial workers, the younger generation, and intellectuals.

Along with reform programs, the National Government implemented a new political agenda that would administer a national authoritative and democratic rule. The goals of the new program included promoting private industries and moving government industries under individual holdings. It discouraged monopolies and formed an industrial system allowing industrial workers to share and have a voice in owning and managing the private industries. The industrial system helped workers through land reforms, water conservation, and land reclamation. The new program promoted the idea of tenant farmers and executing local self-government to conserve civil rights.

Under the national government, the provincial government existed. The federal government managed foreign affairs, national defense, administration, national income, national laws, and international trade policies. The provincial governments directed local self-governments, educational systems, mining, police systems, commerce, agriculture, taxation, industrial systems, and divisions of the bureaucratic sectors. The laws would be proposed and ordinated by the national government, while the provincial government would be directed and managed by the provincial government.[65]

With the U.S. close allies with the Republic of China ("ROC")—the official name for the Nationalist Government in Taiwan under President Chiang Kai-shek—President Truman and his administration hoped to make sure that Taiwan and the ROC would remain independent from the People's Republic of China, the communist government of China.

Several motives incentivized the need to have the ROC continue independently. The main point of most of these incentives centered around the advantages Taiwan posed as a geopolitical and resource asset to the United States, particularly in the war against communism.

---

[65] Wang, Gung-hsing. "Nationalist Government Policies, 1949-1951." *The Annals of the American Academy of Political and Social Science* 277 (1951): 213-23. Accessed January 21, 2020. www.jstor.org/stable/1030267, p. 213-215.

While it did not provide the U.S. with military advantages, Taiwan had the potential to give military benefits to nations hostile towards the U.S. The U.S. also had political influence on Taiwan by suggesting and involving American democratic politics in the ROC. One solution to better sustain their independence involved Taiwan and the ROC being recognized by the United Nations as China.[66] As a United Nations member, and with Taiwan seen as the official Chinese Government, the Republic of China would take actions in political and military affairs that involved the United Nations.

As a legitimate government, the ROC had embassies, diplomatic offices, and 21 consular offices in states that recognized its position. It needed support from the U.S. to maintain its existence as an independent state and to aid the ROC against any attacks or attempted invasion from the Communists; however, the U.S. refused to provide aid to any unprovoked attacks that the ROC might attempt against the mainland.

As a result, friction developed between ROC President Chiang and the U.S. because Chiang vehemently believed that the Communists should be attacked. Chiang was confident that, with the U.S. aid, the Communist government was prime for defeat, thereby reinstating the ROC on the mainland. Chiang's request was refused, and it was finally decided that the ROC military would be used for defensive

---

[66] Van Vranken Hickey, Dennis. "United States Policy and the International Status of Taiwan." *The Journal of East Asian Affairs* 7, no. 2 (1993): 563-86. Accessed January 21, 2020. www.jstor.org/stable/23254199, p. 566-568.

purposes only. In return for the ROC's acceptance of the terms, the U.S. gave billions of dollars of military aid to Taiwan, including arms, a fleet, and military assistance of several thousand soldiers.[67]

While the ROC requested aid from the U.S., it also strengthened its political position with the United Nations, specifically among Western nations, and was given a seat at the U.N. Security Council. The ROC proved its worth through stiff resistance against the Japanese, despite overwhelming military and political disadvantages.

Following the war with the Japanese, the ROC would be one of the founding members of the United Nations. It played a part in drafting the United Nations resolution, written during the Korean War, stating that all U.N. members were to aid any other member or protected country under attack. One of the most critical actions he ROC took as a U.N. member was participating in the signing of Japan's official surrender at the Treaty of San Francisco in 1951, six years after its first treaty putting Japan under American occupation. This principal act demonstrated that the ROC was recognized as the Chinese Government and strengthened the ROC's political power in Taiwan and the Penghu Islands.[68]

---

[67] Quigley, Harold S. "The National Government on Taiwan." In *China's Politics in Perspective*, 162-73. University of Minnesota Press, 1962. Accessed January 22, 2020. www.jstor.org/stable/10.5749/j.ctttspwv.21, p. 167-168.

[68] Tan, S. H. "Representation of China in the United Nations." *The American Journal of International Law* 65, no. 4 (1971): 20-30. Accessed January 22, 2020. www.jstor.org/stable/25660388, p. 20-23.

Chapter 5:

Treatment of Taiwanese under KMT

While the ROC may have strengthened their position on Taiwan economically and politically, their treatment of the native Taiwanese population is synonymous with the treatment of many other Asian native populations under Western colonizers. It is important to understand the relationship between the Taiwanese and Nationalists, particularly the Taiwanese population in China, to understand the cruel and exploitative treatment of Taiwanese by the Nationalist Government upon their establishment of the new Republic of China.

The Taiwanese population in China before 1945 numbered around 100,000. The study of the Taiwanese population is important because it shows an understanding of how the Nationalists treated native Taiwanese following the takeover of Taiwan, as well as Taiwan's political involvement in Taiwan under the Nationalist Government. In China, between 1921 and 1937, many Taiwanese residents formed organizations — primarily anti-Japanese organizations. Following the start of the war with Japan, the Nationalist Party supported many

Taiwanese anti-Japanese wartime organizations. The Taiwan Revolutionary League, while formed by mostly Taiwanese citizens, was closely associated with, and financially supported by, the KMT. The Taiwan Revolutionary League conducted intelligence gathering, military actions, and propaganda. It was followed by other revolutionary organizations such as the Taiwan Volunteers, a political-military group, and the Taiwan Party Headquarters, a section of the Taiwan Party in China.

The Taiwan Revolutionary League, along with the other Taiwanese revolutionary organizations, decided to unite under the Alliance of Taiwanese Revolutionary Organization. Several reasons and outcomes explain why the Taiwanese groups wanted to come from this unification. First, the unification amalgamated the Taiwanese revolutionary organizations and strengthened their presence in China. Second, their increased presence amplified the awareness and concerns that the Chinese Government and population had towards the Taiwanese population. Third, the unification connected the political stance of the Taiwanese revolutionaries.

While the formation of the Alliance of Taiwanese Revolutionary Organization reinforced and supplemented the presence and stance of the Taiwanese revolutionaries, it did not have much support from the non-revolutionary Taiwanese population in China. Also, the effectiveness and efficiency of their work left much to be desired. The goal of the Alliance of Taiwanese Revolution Organization, with the help of Chinese Nationalists, was to unite all Taiwanese revolutionaries in overthrowing the Japanese in China and Taiwan, reclaim Taiwan, and aid China in instituting a new government under certain principles and policies. The Taiwan Revolutionary League emphasized utilizing propaganda to attract more Taiwanese on both the mainland and Taiwan to support their cause. The League wanted to convince foreigners that Taiwan belonged to China, as these Taiwanese had grown accustomed and connected with the mainland after residing there for years. Despite this, the League wanted to educate Chinese authorities on future treatment of postwar Taiwan and to convince the Chinese to view Taiwan as its province, as opposed to an occupied colony. The League committed to holding regular meetings and press conferences, publishing journals, broadcasting their ideas, promoting their cause to the public, and influencing future Chinese policies on postwar Taiwan.

The Taiwanese Volunteer formed a political-military organization with an emphasis on forming an independent military unit under the KMT army. Volunteers were involved in diplomatic and foreign politics, as well as spreading important messages on Taiwan. They also educated soldiers both within the organization and the KMT military to speak Japanese and understand Japanese propaganda. Understanding the Japanese made it easier for volunteers to interrogate prisoners and decipher intercepted messages transmitted between Japanese units and leaders.

In terms of activities and importance, the Taiwanese Party Headquarters had a major political stance in the Nationalist Government because it worked extensively with the Nationalists on Taiwanese issues both on the mainland and in Taiwan. It also had a prominent intelligence network within Japan's military and helped create important contacts within Japanese occupied territory, notably in Taiwan and Hong Kong. They not only sent the Nationalist military important intelligence work, they also recruited Chinese and Taiwanese in the occupied territories to assist their efforts. Unfortunately, since the Taiwanese Party Headquarters worked closely on the frontlines, many of their important party leaders were killed, resulting in the party being forced to the rear and party leaders replaced with non-Taiwanese members, which weakened their position.

During the Cairo Conference of 1943, China, Great Britain, and the U.S. determined that Taiwan, the Penghu Islands, and Manchuria would be given to China. As the war ended and China prepared its reclamation of occupied territories, the League, understanding the gravitas of China's Taiwan plans, hoped to address issues of the Nationalist Government's civil administration and gradual occupation of Taiwan to benefit both the Nationalist Government, Nationalist immigrants, and Taiwanese locals. Following the war, the Nationalist Government created the Central Training Institute to send military-escorted government workers to Taiwan. The workers were expected to take over the government and analyze Taiwan's structure such as their economy, finances, and education to understand Taiwanese social and political stance. They also studied the Japanese colonial administration on Taiwan to analyze the impact and influence Japan had on the

Taiwanese population from half a century of occupation. The Taiwan Cadre Training Camps, which assisted the government workers and escorts with Taiwanese social and political lifestyle, taught Japanese to their volunteers to better read laws and materials written for Taiwan under Japanese colonial rule. The volunteers learned about the political and economic institutions of the Japanese colonial administration, as well as social institutions. The social institutions studied included Taiwanese education, industrial industries, public health, financial institutions, and police institutions.

Despite efforts to convince the Chinese Nationalists otherwise, the Taiwanese failed to relieve Nationalists' views that the Taiwanese were subservient to the Japanese and should be treated as the Nationalists would treat Japanese prisoners. The half-mainland Taiwanese attempted to inform the Chinese about abuse of the Taiwanese population under the Japanese occupation, Taiwanese patriotism, and the Taiwanese experience in local self-government. Nevertheless, the Chinese continued to view the Taiwanese as enemies, instead of compatriots or Chinese until a certain period of education under Chinese institutions. Due to Taiwan's history of uprisings against oppressors, Nationalist leaders believed in strict and intense dominance over the Taiwanese population to prevent reoccurrence of such uprisings.[69]

---

[69] Jacobs, J. Bruce. "Taiwanese and the Chinese Nationalists, 1937-1945: The Origins of Taiwan's "Half-Mountain People" (Banshan Ren)." Modern China 16, no. 1 (1990): 84-118. Accessed January 28, 2020. www.jstor.org/stable/189184, p. 88-107.

Chinese fear of Japanese influence on the Taiwanese population was not an unfounded idea, as seen in the experience of Kay Chen. Kay and her family's experience under Japanese education and influence had a significant effect on their views on the Chinese and Americans. Due to the pro-Japanese impact from Japanese schooling and colonial rule, Kay's brothers and fathers were encouraged to join the military, exposing them to pro-Japanese sentiments and patriotic views. Kay's eldest brother was in the navy; her other brothers joined both the air force and military. Taiwanese suffering from American bombings and the Japanese propaganda spread to the Taiwanese population, leading to anti-Chinese and anti-American sentiments. Kay's family developed deep discrimination against Chinese in part from Japanese slurs.[70]

Kay Chen's Grade School Class. (Courtesy of Ellen Hickman.)

[70] Chen, Kay. Interview by Ellen Hickman. Oral Interview. November 29, 2019.

Raid on Taipei bomb locations[71]

After the Japan's surrender and before the official Nationalist establishment in Taiwan, Nationalists established a Taiwan Provincial Administration to apply Nationalist policies and administrative rule over Taiwan. The Taiwanese found both the Chinese and Japanese governments corrupt and oppressive, but the Nationalist Government was considered more detrimental to Taiwan's political, social, and economic situation, because

---

[71] "File:Taipei bomb.jpg - Wikimedia Commons." https://commons.wikimedia.org/wiki/File:Taipei_bomb.jpg. Accessed 25 Feb. 2020.

of ineffectiveness and inefficiency. One significant contribution to their economic failures was the financial status of Taiwan adopted from the Japanese. When the Nationalists assumed control of Taiwan, they also acquired the damages to Taiwan's industrial and agricultural facilities from American bombings and Japan's war efforts' demands.

Most costs were directed against the maritime industries and surrounding coastal towns, agrarian facilities, particularly in the sugar industry, and the communication and transportation systems. In 1945, agricultural production became ineffective as the Japanese left, because it relied heavily upon Japanese industrial experts and managers. Their rule, while cruel and exploitative, efficiently managed and controlled agricultural production.

Food shortages and unemployment increased from hundreds of thousands of Taiwanese returning from military service, education, labor, merchants, or bureaucratic positions in China and Japan, combined with a deficient food production and scarcity in jobs, and failures to recover the industrial system. The influx of returning Taiwanese caused unemployment from demobilization of returning Taiwanese laborers and soldiers. The Nationalists' situation worsened when American bombings destroyed much of Taiwan's industrial and agricultural industries, but the Nationalists also used Taiwan's resources to maintain the economy and their democratic and administrative hold on China and struggle against Communists.

Nationalist policies also contributed to Taiwan's dilemma, particularly in regards to claiming former Japanese occupied territories for businesses and administration. Upon occupying Taiwan, the Nationalist Government policies focused on annexing Japanese properties in Taiwan, as opposed to assisting the Taiwanese in managing their industries and reclaiming lands previously taken by the Japanese.

According to the Nationalist Government, all Japanese areas belonged to them. This claim led to disagreements and competition between the Nationalists and the Taiwanese. Much of these lands belonged to Taiwanese natives before sold or seized by the Japanese, so they felt the lands were theirs to use. The Taiwanese tried to petition for the return of lands, but failed, increasing tension between the Taiwanese and mainlanders.

In attempting to manage grain and housing sales, the Nationalists were ineffective in increasing grain production and housing growth. Their ineffectiveness proved particularly harmful to the native Taiwanese population. Initial conflicts and issues between the Nationalist Government and the Taiwanese emerged as Nationalist oppressive and manipulative rule over the Taiwanese and a mutually antagonistic attitude.

There was also a rise in diseases in the forms of cholera, malaria, leprosy, and the bubonic plague which spread through Taiwan. The lack of improvement in public health and sanitation led to the increased speed of these widespread epidemics. The Taiwanese blamed the influx of Nationalists and half-mainland Taiwanese population on bringing over these diseases from China.[72]

The Nationalists' dishonesty in promising Taiwanese expression of freedom, notably in print media, was another reason for disintegration of trust and confidence in the Nationalist Government. While the Nationalists promised freedom of the press, the Taiwanese newspapers expressed criticism towards the Nationalist Government. As a result, the Nationalist Government began restricting newspapers from Taiwanese newspapers which affected the faith and reliance that the Taiwanese had on the government.[73]

Developing conflicts between the Taiwanese and mainlanders evolved from the Nationalist Government corruption and the loss of Taiwanese political power. Following the Japanese colonial administration, the Taiwan Provincial Administration restructured its political system to mirror Japan's political system. When the Nationalist Government arrived, 36,000 Taiwanese lost their jobs to Nationalist officials who took over the administration. The Nationalists seized and dominated political and police structures, applying policies that disproportionately negatively affected the Taiwanese. The Nationalists' treatment of Taiwanese locals may be explained by their views of Taiwanese as Japanese collaborators.

---

[72] Phillips, Steven E. Between Assimilation and Independence: The Taiwanese Encounter Nationalist China, 1945-1950. Stanford, CA: Stanford University Press, 2003, p. 65-66.

[73] Ibid, 69.

A nationwide uprising, known as the 2-28 Incident, originated in Taipei as a dispute between the police and Taiwanese smuggling cigarettes, considered contraband. The disagreement resulted in violence and the death of a nonparticipant. Immediately following the incident, thousands of Taiwanese marched against the Monopoly Bureau Headquarters, provincial administrations, and police departments. The protest led to the military firing into crowds, followed by vandalism. Citizens demonstrated against unemployment, inflation, corruption, unfair treatment by the police, and food shortages. The Taipei uprisings spread and influenced protests and revolts across the nation. In response, the Nationalist Government committed its military and police to suppressing insurgents and even bribed Taiwanese to turn over the agitators.

While sporadic and independent, the various protests and uprisings shared similar goals. There was a unity among revolutionaries, particularly in the provincial government, which had Taiwanese officials who formed a resolution committee. The committee drafted the General Outline listing thirty-two military and political reform demands from the Nationalist administration. The first requested overhaul was to give the Taiwanese complete provincial control.

The uprisings were entirely suppressed on March 8, 1947. A general study revealed that 10,000 Taiwanese were killed with another 30,000 wounded. The Nationalists believed that anti-Chinese and anti-Nationalist sentiments influenced the antagonism, cultivated by decades of Japanese education, propaganda, and Communist influence. This belief prompted the Nationalists to want to wipe away all traces of Japanese influence.

Taipei Branch of the Bureau of Monopoly was occupied by Taiwanese rioters. 1947[74]

The Nationalist Party prohibited Japanese-language publications and records. They also confiscated Japanese uniforms, flags, and other memorabilia under the Japanese colonial period. The Nationalists conducted a decolonization movement from the belief that the Taiwanese natives were distorted and defected from Japanese influence, causing the uprisings and aggressive actions. The end of the decade would lead to the Taiwanese failing to gain more autonomy and, instead, Nationalist centraliz-

[74] 228 Incident, http://www.kmt.org.tw/epaper/_Upload/930226/B2.jpg, https://commons.wikimedia.org/wiki/File:228_Incident_h.jpg.

ing their government in Taiwan to the point of taking over the local governments.[75]

The importance of the Nationalists' treatment of the Taiwanese and their inability to effectively manage the native population and the political, social, and economic situation in Taiwan would lead to their loss of political power both in Taiwan and internationally.

[75] Ibid, 77-88.

Chapter 6:

New Taiwanese National Identity

One of the most momentous ROC years was 1971. The Republic of China in Taiwan had its economic growth and political power increased and supported by the U.N. The bulk of support for Taiwan came from Japan and the U.S. While there has been an increase in growth due to the support, there has also been increased debate for removing Taipei from the U.N. Assembly in the hopes of encouraging the politically powerful People's Republic of China ("PRC") to join the U.N.

In early 1971, President Richard Nixon lifted the travel and trade bans with China, and officially acknowledged and recognized the PRC. That year would build on the U.S. and China relationship through proposing international trade, sending journalists, and even organizing sporting competitions, most notably table tennis.

Nixon sent Secretary of State and National Security Advisor, Henry Kissinger, to open diplomatic talks with Premier of the PRC, Chou En-lai. Due to Japan's reliance and support from the U.S., Taiwan lost a lot of support, but Japan hoped to incorporate both Taipei and Beijing as members of the U.N. Unfortunately, when the votes went through in October 1971, the ROC was officially expelled, and the PRC accepted into the U.N.[76]

The United Nations supported the PRC over the ROC for several reasons. For one, the ROC had little political power and lacked diplomatic influence. While the U.S. wanted to protect Taiwan from communist influences after 1949, the end of the Chinese Cultural Revolution led to China having improved economic and political opportunities for the U.S.

However, the PRC wanted Taiwan to be recognized as a part of China. As such, Taiwan would not be recognized as an independent government and China would be recognized as a single government. The loss of recognition from the U.S. and the U.N. led to Taiwan losing its international position and the rise of opposing political positions to the Nationalists.

The PRC, instead of attempting to forcibly reunify Taiwan with China and risking military engagements, created policies for a single country—but under two government systems. While publicly Taiwan would be recognized as part of China, it would be allowed to keep its political, economic, and social systems, as well as maintain its own military and currency. On the other hand, Taiwan would no longer be recognized by the U.N. as an independent government.[77]

---

[76] Appleton, Sheldon L. "Taiwan: The Year It Finally Happened." *Asian Survey* 12, no. 1 (1972): 32-37. Accessed February 11, 2020. doi:10.2307/2642917, p. 32-33.

[77] Moody, Peter R. "The Democratization of Taiwan and the Reunification of China." *The Journal of East Asian Affairs* 5, no. 1 (1991): 144-84. Accessed February 12, 2020. www.jstor.org/stable/23254084, p. 151-158.

The loss of political power and support for the Nationalist Government from the U.S. led to an increase in native Taiwanese political opposition movements against the ROC. The 1980s saw a growth of organized native Taiwanese movements to encourage the recognition of rights of the native population.

In 1984, the Alliance of Taiwan Aboriginals ("ATA") was established to promote more social services and political recognition for natives. The ATA and its Aboriginal Rights Movement ("ARM") was supported by native Taiwanese university students. Strategies implemented by ARM included assisting urban natives facing social and political discrimination, raising awareness for recognizing native population rights, and protesting issues the natives faced under the KMT.

A national sense of identity and consciousness would grow from these active movements that promoted increased rights and recognition for the native Taiwanese population. Through active protests and movements, the ATA was granted equal citizenship rights and political recognition. In its dispute with the Nationalist Government, the ATA demanded a new Constitution that would allow for native land rights and self-government.[78] The ATA and ARM successfully established a political party known as the Democratic Progressive Party ("DPP"), which advocated for the promotion and protection of

---

[78] Ku, Kun-hui. "Rights to Recognition: Minority/Indigenous Politics in the Emerging Taiwanese Nationalism." *Social Analysis: The International Journal of Social and Cultural Practice* 49, no. 2 (2005): 99-121. Accessed February 14, 2020. www.jstor.org/stable/23178874, p. 102-110.

the native rights, including freedom of speech, press, and thought. It also wanted to prohibit the intervention of political parties in security and military affairs or ownership of government property. The main goal of the DPP was to abolish the corruption and authoritative laws of the KMT towards the native population.[79]

In 1988, the DPP held multiple seminars nationwide to provoke conversation for Taiwanese independence. The platform would be called, "The People Have the Right to Advocate the Independence of Taiwan." While this platform inspired pro-independence motivation, it also caused tension and concerns with the main government. The animosity with the main government might hinder the independence movement more than help due to the government's power to ban the party. A 1988 editorial claimed that, instead of pushing for independence through their platform, the DPP should be more engaged in democratic movements and find land to better settle indigenous people both on the mainland and Taiwan.[80]

The DPP competed with the KMT in the Legislative Yuan, the legislature of the Taiwanese Government, for a political space for native politicians to endorse a more public and political voice in favor of the aboriginal com-

[79] "Political Platform of the Democratic Progressive Party." *World Affairs* 155, no. 3 (1993): 135-38. Accessed February 15, 2020. www.jstor.org/stable/20672354, p. 135-136.

[80] "Editorial 12: "Some Sincere Admonitions for the Democratic Progressive Party," 9 April 1988." *Asian Affairs* 27, no. 3 (2000): 168-70. Accessed February 23, 2020. www.jstor.org/stable/30172786, p. 168-170.

munity. Indigenous legislators gained a prominent number of seats in the Yuan and native legislators would gain their representation in Taiwan's political atmosphere.

In 1997, both KMT and DPP legislators discussed constitutional reformation proposing to cut government spending and increase their effectiveness. The indigenous rights activists felt that engaging in multi-party politics would be most effective in granting and preserving indigenous land and economic rights. The indigenous rights political movement ignited and grew throughout the 1990s through the formation of an aboriginal congress and increased national political representation. Taiwan, which presented national public rituals, began to feature more indigenous culture and incorporated indigenous music in national celebrations. The rise in political and cultural representation and recognition resulted in political power gradually transferring from the KMT to the DPP.[81]

The DPP's political and social progress and the Taiwanese indigenous population would lead to a historic and emblematic moment for the aboriginal community. In 2000, Chen Shu-bian became the first president from the DPP. The KMT consistently lost local elections, but Chen's success showed a growing support for Taiwanese independence and indigenous recognition.[82] The rise in indigenous support can further be understood by Chen

---

[81] Ku, Kun-hui. "Rights to Recognition", p. 114-115.

[82] Rigger, Shelley. "The Democratic Progressive Party in 2000: Obstacles and Opportunities." *The China Quarterly*, no. 168 (2001): 944-59. Accessed February 23, 2020. www.jstor.org/stable/3657366, p. 944.

also winning the mayor of Taipei election against a KMT opponent in 1994.

Several positions that earned Chen more support than others promoting independence was his promise to build on a sea-and-air link with the mainland and inclination to build on Taiwan's relationship with China as an independent nation. The confidence in Chen to improve and maintain Taiwan-China relations, if Taiwan could be deemed independent, improved his popularity. Unfortunately, China did not trust Chen or his positions. Chen hoped to gain Chinese confidence by articulating that he would not claim Taiwan as independent, or interfere with China's National Unification Guidelines for Taiwan, as long as China does not engage militarily against Taiwan. Chen also lessened KMT restrictions on Taiwanese companies' investments in China. Even though Chen became the first president from the DPP, the KMT still held the majority of legislative seats, making it difficult to conduct policies opposing KMT views.[83]

Chen faced many challenges during his administration. First, Chen had tension with China and cross-Strait relations due to his party's desire and aspiration to declare Taiwan as independent. Second, Chen's economic policies to abandon Taiwan's Nuclear Power Plant and to increase budget spending on welfare and environmental projects were ill-prepared and poorly timed, causing a

[83] Wu, Yu-Shan. "Taiwan in 2000 Managing the Aftershocks from Power Transfer." *Asian Survey* 41, no. 1 (2001): 40-48. Accessed February 24, 2020. doi:10.1525/as.2001.41.1.40, p. 41-45.

major public backlash from the rise of electricity prices and power shortages. This lowered the trust and confidence from foreign companies with the DPP's obligation to long-term contracts, due to shutting down power plants for environmental reasons. The final challenge was Chen and the DPP's political tension with the KMT. While the DPP successfully elected a member as president for the first time, he still had to compete with the KMT-majority legislature certain to object and dispute policies or issues that the DPP wanted to address. This obstruction and divided government made it difficult for Chen to be an effective political contributor.[84]

---

[84] Ibid., p. 47-48.

Conclusion

This book covered the history of Taiwan, from the possible first immigrants from China to one of its first aboriginal presidents. The native population faced difficulties and oppression from colonialism, which dramatically altered demographics, economics, and politics. Taiwan's importance in the international geopolitical sphere grew immensely as major economically and politically influential countries, including China, Japan, and European countries, discovered the island's agricultural and economic benefits. Taiwan, originally known by European countries as Formosa, started as a trading center between Asian and European countries. European colonial expansion hegemonized the island, along with many other Asian countries, which furthered its economic, industrial, and agricultural interests. It would ultimately assume the name "Taiwan" after the Chinese reclaimed the island.

While an important asset to many countries, only after the Japanese fully colonized and exploited Taiwan to advance its industrial and economic productivity and integrate the natives into their work force, Taiwan began to be seen as a more relevant state in the geopolitical atmosphere due to its geographical location and agricultural, industrial and economic potentials. When Nationalist China was losing to their Communist counterparts and the U.S. sought potential refuges to establish a separate democratic, anti-communist government for potentially retaking China, Taiwan became a key location thanks to its remoteness from China, and strategic and economic importance.

While foreign governments and merchants exploited Taiwan for economic and political benefits, they failed to understand their impact on aboriginals. Before Japan colonized Taiwan at the end of 19th century, colonizers from the Netherlands, Portugal, and China either attempted to convert the natives towards their own religion, cohabitate with them for trade, or abolished them in order to use their lands for their own purposes. Upon colonizing Taiwan, Japan's approach shifted to assimilating and integrating the native population into their own culture, as well as using natives in the labor force to increase Japan's economic and industrial production rates.

Under the Japanese and KMT, Taiwanese natives faced persecution, oppression, and violence, most notably the 2-28 Incident involving the KMT military and violent retaliation from the Japanese against villages that aided or were involved in anti-Japanese guerilla actions.

This book is an effort to understand why Taiwan transformed into its current importance on the world stage and to use that knowledge to understand the treatment of the native population—an issue very rarely discussed in Taiwan's history. The book intends to raise awareness of the history of oppression of native populations under foreign nations.

Printed in Great Britain
by Amazon